# HURRICANE

# HURRICANE
## THE PLANE THAT WON THE WAR

## JACKY HYAMS

Michael O'Mara Books Limited

The paperback edition first published in 2024
First published in Great Britain in 2023 by
Michael O'Mara Books Limited
9 Lion Yard
Tremadoc Road
London SW4 7NQ

A CIP catalogue record for this book is available from the British Library.

This product is made of material from well-managed, FSC®-certified
forests and other controlled sources. The manufacturing processes
conform to the environmental regulations of the country of origin.

ISBN: 978-1-78929-684-6 in paperback print format
ISBN: 978-1-78929-490-3 in ebook format

1 2 3 4 5 6 7 8 9 10

Designed and typeset by Claire Cater
Printed and bound by CPI Group (UK) Ltd, Croydon, CR0 4YY

www.mombooks.com

# CONTENTS

# FOREWORD

## AUGUST 2022

**M**Y HEART IS POUNDING IN MY CHEST as I walk towards our new visitor – a visitor that would have been a common sight at RAF Westhampnett during the summer of 1940 when 145 Squadron was resident with its Hawker Hurricanes. Today, the now gently hissing and ticking beast standing on the apron at Goodwood Airfield is a very welcome sight.

Her pilot slides back the canopy and steps down the wing to meet the ground crew, ready for fuelling and readying for the next sortie, a formation flight over England's south coast in conjunction with her stablemate, our Spitfire.

We climb up to the cockpit and clean the canopies, readying her for flight, just as the ground crew would have done when Goodwood was an RAF station all those years ago.

It clearly displays its Hawker lineage and looks, but what a thing of beauty! She is sturdy, robust; it looks right and surely flies right. Her undercarriage is wide and gives you an idea that she is more directionally stable on take-off.

You climb the external step up to the wing and into the 'office'. It is roomy and the visibility from the cockpit looks reassuringly better than that of the Spitfire. She is an absolutely fabulous aircraft and much admired by all who gaze upon her, standing higher than the Spitfire Mk IX parked adjacent to her – the resident fighters that normally take the limelight at Goodwood.

This lovingly restored Battle of Britain, Hurricane UP-W, R4118 of 605 Squadron is attracting attention from all corners of the airfield, pilots and ground crew alike.

For today she is a rare bird and many who witness her see her as the poor cousin of the Spitfire – for all the wrong reasons.

She deserves to be recognized as the fighter that was more prolific and achieved more victories against the Luftwaffe than the Spitfire. She was the workhorse, but sadly over the years 'Spitfire snobbery' has remained.

Luftwaffe pilots, when shot down, all claimed they had been victims of the RAF's newest fighter, the Spitfire. But in reality it was probably and more likely to be the Hawker Hurricane – with its stable gun platform that could hold its own in a turning fight. With its fabric fuselage, it could also take more damage, as cannon shells passed through them, meaning that the plane could subsequently be repaired, returning to the fray. She was loved by her pilots for her ruggedness, and they adapted their tactics to suit the advantage of the aircraft design, enabling them to get the better of any Bf 109 pilot who dared try and out-turn the Hurricane.

She was ubiquitous and her influence was felt in nearly every theatre of war during the Second World War. A night fighter, ground-attack aircraft, tank or even boat buster, she was quite an adaptable aircraft, but sadly did not lend herself to as many changes and upgrades as her sister, the Supermarine Spitfire. Her role in achieving air superiority, supporting ground troops and changing the course of the war, however, should never be forgotten.

As an aviation historian, I relish every day of being able to work with these remarkable planes. Each day we work with them, we are accompanied by the ghosts of the pilots and ground crew who worked with and loved their aircraft.

We must continue to tell their stories and pass them on to the next generation. It is key also that we remember the contribution of the designers, factory workers and delivery pilots to the outcome of the Second World War.

It is a privilege to be able to write a foreword for this book, celebrating and remembering the achievements of all involved with such a special aircraft.

*Mark Hillier*
*Aviation Historian and Head of Operations*
*Spitfires.com, Goodwood Airfield*

# A NOTE FROM
# THE AUTHOR

IT IS THE YOUTH OF THE AIRMEN that remains, lingering in the mind's eye, down the years.

They stay with you these young aviators, many barely beyond their teens, long after the black day of Britain's fight for survival in 1940 has passed into history.

Each year in November, multitudes across the world stand briefly silent to remember and pay homage to those millions who have represented their country in many different wars, a silent tribute to their valiant endeavour. This book, too, is a tribute to their courage and valour – and their passionate belief in their cause.

I once asked the esteemed Spitfire hero, the late Geoff Wellum, a teenager when he climbed into his Spitfire for the first time, if he believed that today's generation would sign up so willingly to face the fire.

'Yes,' he said without hesitation. 'I do believe the youngsters today would do it.'

I was shocked. Do we still have a generation of courageous and determined young men prepared to face extinction to defend these islands? Journalists are renowned cynics, so I must give credence to one who believed this to be true.

I am fortunate enough to have penned previous memoirs of Britain's wartime story. Yet strangely, this one, the history of the Hawker Hurricane, whose aviators achieved a perilous victory in the midst of chaos, is strangely different.

The fragility of their endeavour, hanging on an awesomely fine thread, has already been recorded countless times, yet there still remains an excellent reason to celebrate this aeroplane from so long ago: the Hawker Hurricane never really gained the deserved wartime accolades accorded to the Supermarine Spitfire; to this very day some believe the Spitfire was the lone British fighter in the skies during those four turbulent months of the Battle of Britain.

One aspect of this book is to re-examine the Hawker Hurricane, its role during the battle as well as those young men who arrived in Britain from all over the world to seek freedom and reject tyranny everywhere.

Many, of course, came from countries now no longer part of Britain's long-ago Empire. Some from those that had already faced the Nazi onslaught, carrying with them an inward fire of determination to fight back, no matter what the cost. Many, too, had simply volunteered from far and wide because they wanted to join the fight.

This book highlights the stories of some of these young men from across the world simply because, in many cases, their stories of courage and determination are awe inspiring, though often tragic. The Hurricane's history straddled the globe: it extended to Malta, Russia, the Western Desert, Burma (now Myanmar) – far-flung places on the world's map. Twenty-five air forces around the world saw service with the Hurricane.

Yet there were other accompanying heroes too: those men whose extraordinary vision and talent created the Hawker Hurricane in the first place. Equal contribution must be handed to the Hurri's dedicated ground teams, travelling all over the world alongside the RAF squadrons. Their endeavour illuminates the story from their similarly perilous perspective.

There is a certain glamour attached to aviation and war – one good reason why the Spitfire, in traditional memory, remained the sleek, fast thoroughbred of wartime, and the Hurricane – the stubby one; the reliable, resilient warhorse – was accorded lesser significance. Yet peer a shade deeper into its story in those far-off days of the Second World War and a closer, significant truth emerges to reveal why the Hurricane's story is so important – and why its history must now reverberate across the generations.

I have written this book for those who may already know some history of the Hurricane, as well as for those approaching it from a very limited understanding or with none at all, who perhaps may only have encountered fragments of their families' Second World War history through anecdotes, photos or documents passed on from grandparents, distant uncles, cousins or relatives who recorded their own wartime histories down the decades. Each and every family everywhere has its own personal story of war and remembrance.

The story of the 'Hurri' is a tribute to a long-ago past. Yet it reveals much that remains hugely relevant to the present: a tale of business acumen, youthful courage, resolve, camaraderie, skill in the air and solid, unflinching determination. All these are the attributes of a beloved fighter plane – and of those involved, directly or indirectly, with its story.

*Jacky Hyams*

# INTRODUCTION

THE HAWKER HURRICANE WAS A BRITISH SINGLE-SEATER fighter aircraft. The 'Hurri', as it is often affectionately known, shot down more enemy planes than the Spitfire during the Battle of Britain in 1940. More than half of the 1,200 German aircraft over the course of the battle were shot down by the Hawker Hurricane.

The Spitfire garnered much of the glory as a fighter plane, the 'public face' of the RAF during the Battle of Britain. Yet it was the Hurricane that was the authentic 'warhorse' of British Second World War aviation history.

The Hawker Hurricane was rugged, less expensive to build than the Spitfire, and far more easily and swiftly repaired. So the more workmanlike Hurricane deserves all the plaudits. The furious battle in the air that defeated Germany's attempts to invade Britain in the summer of 1940 would not have been won without the Hurri. In fact, the Hurricane and Spitfire were a great double act. When operating together, as they frequently did in the Battle of Britain, they formed a partnership no other air force could match.

At the time of the battle, the RAF could call on thirty-two squadrons of Hurricanes and nineteen squadrons of Spitfires, easily making the Hurri the dominant British fighter. Here was a plane that could withstand more than a few hits from the enemy – and, though battered, continue to fly. The Spitfire was superb and had a faster performance in the air. However, the Hurri was much stronger. In the momentous battle for the survival of Britain, its very resilience made a huge difference.

'It literally saved the country,' said Royal Navy test pilot Eric 'Winkle' Brown (1919–2016). He knew. He had flown more aircraft types than anyone else in the world.

Closer examination of the Hurricane's history reveals other important aspects of its 'warhorse' signature beyond those perilous weeks of the summer of 1940.

Yet even today, the very question of 'which fighter won the war' divides studies concerning the Battle of Britain. One good reason why the Hurricane has tended to receive less attention than the Spitfire is relatively simple: glamour. Britain fell madly in love with the Supermarine Spitfire immediately. It dominated the nation's front pages once war was declared in 1939, a fantastically good-looking icon right from the start.

The Hurricane, with its chunky design, stability and steady platform – making it easier to handle – has not been widely perceived in the same way, despite it being the first-ever 300 mph (483 km/h) aircraft designed for the RAF. Notwithstanding, then, its superior track record – it having been deployed successfully in every theatre of the Second World War – it has never received the same accolades.

Furthermore, the Hawker Hurricane's attributes have remained somewhat less obvious. Aviation, now and then, demands vast military expenditure – and during the 1930s a reluctance to countenance that war with Nazi Germany was looming led to the British Government's blinkered anti-war stance.

As a consequence, the British aviation industry had spent

very little on military aircraft development for quite some time. Aviation itself, a novelty to the general public in the early twentieth century, had played a part during the First World War, and when this ended, in 1918, the RAF was the most powerful air force in the world. Yet when hostilities ceased then, a hundred and eighty-five RAF squadrons were reduced to twenty-eight, with just seven based in the UK.

In Germany, once Hitler and the Nazi Party took power in 1933, an organized programme was underway to develop brand-new aircraft to lead the world in military aviation. Fighter planes like the Heinkel 70 (He 70) and the Messerschmitt 109 (Me 109) would go on to dominate aerial combat in the early years of the Second World War.

Any attempt to keep the German rearmament programme clandestine had gone by the end of 1933. Leading German aeronautical companies, including Heinkel, Dornier, Junkers and Messerschmitt, were encouraged to develop military bombers and fighters for the Luftwaffe. In Britain, awareness – let alone encouragement – of the need to build military aviation was merely germinating – frighteningly slow to lead to the constructing of any form of airborne defence of the country.

At Britain's Air Ministry, senior officials believed in the past. So the two-seater biplane (which had two sets of wings stacked on top of each other), once the staple of RAF squadrons, remained the preference. Even as late as the summer of 1937, just two years before the declaration of the Second World War, all RAF squadrons were flying these planes. Only when it became glaringly, unmistakably obvious that Adolf Hitler was openly creating a mighty war machine did the need for brand-new fast monoplane fighter planes (single-seaters), crucial for Britain's defence, sink in. By then, the older biplanes *had* to be replaced by the modern monoplane (with just one set of wings).

As reality dawned, so came realization of the need to build the new fighters quickly. It made an important difference that the Hawker Hurricane was significantly cheaper to build than the Spitfire. (It took 10,000 man-hours to produce; a Spitfire 15,000.) Just as importantly, as indicated earlier, the Hurricane was often much easier to repair.

The construction of the Hawker Hurricane was based on previous aircraft built by Hawker Aviation; specifically, an evolution of the earlier Hawker Fury. This meant that producing a brand-new fighter plane for RAF service squadrons – some of which were already experienced in working with and repairing a plane similar in construction to the Hurricane – was considerably easier. The simplicity of its design and conventional wing layout meant a remarkably fast turnaround on the ground when the aircraft needed repair. By then, when aerial combat was a harsh reality, every minute counted.

The Hurri's success in 1940 during the spectacular air battles fought over the English coast – the biggest air raid ever seen in the country – remains a hugely significant part of Britain's island history. On 15 September 1940, the RAF shot down a record number of 180 planes – a mere handful of airmen defending civilization.

The Hawker Hurricane story does not rest there. During the Second World War, the plane served as a day fighter, night fighter, bomber interceptor, ground-attack aircraft, the first-ever rocket-launched fighter, and an early tank buster – and as the Sea Hurricane with the Royal Navy, launched in 1941.

In the first days of the war in 1940, during the 'Phoney War' period of relative calm in Britain, Hurricane squadrons were despatched to support Britain's French allies in what is known as the Battle of France. During Operation Dynamo in 1940 (the evacuation of British, French and Belgian troops cut off by the German Army in Dunkirk), Hawker Hurricanes were there, operating from British bases. In 1941, they helped deliver the Mediterranean island of Malta from invasion. In jungle combat and in the deserts of North Africa late in 1941, Hurricanes also served as ground-attack aircraft, far better suited to rough terrain than the more fragile Spitfire.

By the time their production ended in 1944, 14,487 Hawker Hurricanes had fought during wartime. Many had been delivered to Allied forces around the world. Three thousand flew from airfields in the north of Russia, protecting Arctic convoys.

History will continue to look back and ponder over innumerable documented accounts. But in this case, a closer examination of the story shows that, from beginning to end, the 'Hurri' richly deserves to be far more widely celebrated as the hero of aviation's 'finest hour'.

This truly can be described as the plane that won the war.

# CHAPTER 1

# BIRTH OF A FIGHTER

## FEBRUARY 1936: A VISIT TO MUNICH

FRANK MURDOCH (1904–96) IS HURRYING AWAY from Munich's Central Station towards his hotel, the magnificent Bayerischer Hof, right in the heart of Munich's Old Town.

Murdoch, an aeronautical engineer, is reaching the end of a four-day trip to Germany. Earlier this afternoon he finalized the contract for his key assignment on the trip: a visit to the vast MAN manufacturing and engineering factory located in the nearby university town of Augsburg. A well-travelled man, Murdoch cannot help but be impressed by certain aspects of Munich: the grand classical nineteenth-century buildings, the opera house, the beautiful English garden, the famous art collections. Briefly, he has found time to take in one of the many beer houses proliferating everywhere.

Frank's main mission at MAN was to secure an order for a superb new diesel engine on behalf of his close friend and boss, millionaire Sir Thomas Sopwith, Chairman of Hawker Aircraft – one of Britain's largest aviation manufacturing companies, founded in 1912. The men share an absorbing passion for ocean racing and Sopwith wants the new engine for his new luxury diesel yacht, *Philante*, which will eventually become one of the finest private yachts afloat. Yet Murdoch's visit to Germany for the new engine has turned out to be a far more eye-opening sojourn than the two men might have anticipated.

Escorted around the MAN factory, Murdoch noted the large numbers of U-boat engines currently under construction. And one of the company's engineers also arranged for him to visit the Heinkel aircraft factory, where production was similarly booming. He already knew that in this part of Germany he was at the very epicentre of the National Socialist Party, with the town's imposing stone structure, the Brown House, hosting the HQ of Adolf Hitler's Nazi Party.

Just three years earlier, Adolf Hitler had turned Germany's once fragile democracy into a one-party dictatorship of extreme nationalism, militarism, racism and anti-Semitism. Hitler's newly enacted laws – excluding all Jews, Blacks, Gypsies and homosexuals as well as other minority groups – have been dramatically changing Germany, its people, its culture and much that went before.

In March 1933, just a few miles outside Munich, the concentration camp of Dachau opened, initially housing political prisoners. Dachau was an early forerunner of many more notorious Nazi-controlled concentration camps, the death camps whose legacy of torture, unspeakable medical experiments and planned extermination of millions in gas chambers would only be fully revealed to the world after the Nazi defeat in 1945.

Back home in Britain, certain aspects of Nazi Germany had been reported in the newspapers. Yet most had said very little about the startlingly harsh reality of Nazi control. Britain's newspaper barons of the 1930s had, in the main, remained very much in line with the British Government's appeasement policy. Britain's politicians – and its people – wanted to avoid, if at all possible, any thought of a second devastating war with Germany, just two decades after the end of the First World War in 1918.

Yet what Murdoch witnessed on his trip must have rung alarm bells. In Munich, he could see for himself the reality of what was now taking place in the heart of Nazi Germany. Out on the streets, uniformed stormtroopers and SS men in their heavy black boots and black uniforms were everywhere, while huge tanks and military armoured cars repeatedly rumbled by.

The evidence was overwhelming: a massive Nazi build-up of armaments and military equipment was taking place. Hitler was preparing a mighty war machine for Germany – with no discernible effort at any kind of concealment. Frank Murdoch could see very clearly what was about to be unleashed in Europe and the world. Yet at home, it seemed as if Britain still remained in denial of Hitler's aims: sleepwalking towards unthinkable disaster.

Throughout the 1930s one lone voice, that of MP Winston Churchill, spoke out in the British Parliament warning of German rearmament – and Britain's pitiful lack of military strength. Time and again Churchill warned of the dangers inherent in the rise of Nazi Germany – the 'brown plague', as committed anti-fascists in Europe were already describing it. Mostly, Churchill was ignored: those around him in the political spectrum remained focused on appeasement, not war. British diplomacy, it was believed, could keep everything under control – even Herr Hitler.

Frank Murdoch realizes that he needs to inform Sopwith, his boss, of everything he has learned in Munich. The two men had already suspected what Hitler and the Nazis might be planning. But now the stark truth is there – for all to see.

As he settles down on the train taking him back to England that evening, Murdoch – who works in the design office of Hawker Aviation – wastes no time in compiling a very detailed report of his trip, outlining everything he has witnessed. He knows very well that the wealthy, far-sighted Sopwith will immediately understand that speed of action is now overwhelmingly imperative – and how important it is to start to produce a brand-new fighter plane.

Sopwith's company (previously known as H. G. Hawker Engineering, before becoming Hawker Aircraft in 1934) is already an industry leader. It designed and built most of the aircraft flown by the RAF during the early 1930s. Yet Britain's aviation authority, known as the Air Ministry, has, so far, proved reluctant to swiftly develop existing plans to build new fighters.

Whatever the official policy, Britain urgently needs thousands of new fighter planes to be constructed as rapidly as possible. The situation is potentially desperate: all-out war with Germany could threaten the country's very survival.

In March 1936, just a couple of weeks after the Munich trip, Sir Thomas Sopwith instructs Hawker's planning department to commence scheduling production of 1,000 new fighter planes. Their speed, over 300 mph (483 km/h), would be twice as fast as anything built for the First World War.

There is an existing provisional contract for Hawker to build 600 brand-new fighter planes: the Hawker Hurricane. It has not yet been signed off by the Air Ministry. But Sopwith has given the go-ahead for production of a thousand of the new aircraft because he correctly assumes that export orders would most likely cover any excess over existing RAF orders. A shrewd, talented, well-connected man, with a team of dedicated aviation workers and designers, headed by Sydney Camm, Sopwith is convinced that a swift commercial gamble will pay off.

Without a single firm order on the books, Hawker Aviation has immediately 'tooled up' at their state-of-the-art production factory – still reaching completion – at Langley, near Slough, gearing up to start production of the new fighter.

The gamble pays off. In June 1936, the contract ordering the construction of the 600 planes is signed off by the Air Ministry – the largest production order, thus far, to be placed for military aircraft during peacetime.

By then another new fast fighter aircraft had also been approved for the RAF, the Air Ministry having placed an order for 310 Supermarine Spitfires in June 1936. The Spitfire was in production at Supermarine's facility at Woolston, near Southampton, but early-stage Spitfire production was slow to build up; 200 more Spitfires were ordered by the Ministry in March 1938. In 1940 – after the Second World War had been declared – 1,246 new airworthy Spitfires were delivered to the RAF, against the 2,521 Hurricanes already delivered in the same period.

Britain's Air Ministry had also considered a third single-engine fighter aircraft for their front-line home defence: the Boulton Paul Defiant. The Defiant was a two-seat fighter with a four-gun rotating dorsal turret. It had no forward-firing armament, so it could not shoot down enemy aircraft from behind. The early Defiant turret allowed the gunner to rotate directly forward and transfer firing control of the gun to the pilot. Its ability to fire perpendicular to the fuselage initially had the element of surprise.

The Nazi air bombardment of the town of Guernica in Spain on 26 April 1937 caused over 1,600 civilian deaths. This news spread fear that aerial bombing could devastate cities – and kill ordinary civilians. An official Air Ministry order was made for 67 Boulton Paul Defiants just two days after the Guernica tragedy: the aircraft was ordered straight from the drawing board even without a prototype. A further 202 Defiant Mark Is were ordered in February 1938 and another 150 in December 1938, raising the total of Defiants to 600.

The Defiant eventually flew at Dunkirk and the Battle of Britain. Initially it was successful as the Germans had no idea that the RAF had a fighter that could fire to the rear. But once the Luftwaffe pilots got their measure, the Defiant's glory days were over. The Defiants then became death traps for their crews, incapable of dogfighting, and they became far too slow in getting away from the incoming enemy. Many pilots later complained that it was also a difficult task in bailing out of a stricken aircraft and many had to go down with their planes.

It was eventually withdrawn from daylight operations on 28 August 1940.

Production of the new Hawker Hurricane turned out to be slower than originally planned by six months, following the decision to refit the plane with the high-performance Merlin II engine (the Merlin I was not proving altogether reliable). It was later claimed that the newly built Hurricane might have benefited from the six-month delay, as it turned out to be slightly faster than it would otherwise have been with a Merlin I engine.

## THE FIRST FLIGHT

Alongside Sir Thomas Sopwith and his friend Frank Murdoch, full credit for the Hurricane's existence must be shared with Hawker Aircraft designer Sir Sydney Camm.

The best outcomes are frequently a result of teamwork: the

combination of Sopwith's shrewd foresight and business acumen merged with Camm's passion for aviation design confirm that premise. What more, then, do we know of these two men?

## SIR THOMAS SOPWITH (1888–1989)

Sir Thomas Octave Murdoch Sopwith, CBE, was an aviation pioneer and entrepreneur *par excellence*. When his company was absorbed into British Aerospace in 1977 it owned half of Britain's entire aircraft industry. Often described as a hunting, shooting, fishing and sailing man, Sopwith would take calculated risks in business whenever necessary.

Born in Kensington, London, the only son of eight children, his father was a civil engineer and the family were well off. At age ten, on a family holiday in Scotland, a gun lay across young Thomas's knee. It accidentally went off. It killed his father. The experience marked the schoolboy for life.

'Tommy' Sopwith was not, in any way, academic. Schooling ended at the age of thirteen. He later joined an engineering college, Seafield Park, near Portsmouth. Initially he worked in the motor trade but by 1910 he had developed an intense fascination with early aviation. This led to him buying his first monoplane. He taught himself how to fly it. Very soon he was a professional aviator, giving exhibition flights and joyrides, competing in air displays in America, making a name for himself in the early aviation world.

At twenty-four, he started the Sopwith School of Flying in Brooklands, Surrey. Here he met Australian trainee pilot Harry Hawker and gave early flying lessons to Hugh Trenchard – who would later be known as 'the father of the RAF'.

By 1913, Sopwith made his first foray into aircraft

manufacture. Sopwith Aviation was created in Kingston, Surrey, alongside Harry Hawker and Fred Sigrist. Both played an important role: aviator Hawker was an ideas man, Sigrist a highly intuitive engineer.

In August 1914, when the First World War started, the British aircraft industry was small – yet the Sopwith company already had seven aircraft available for war service. A new factory was built at Canbury Park Road, Kingston. These were early years for aviation production. But as Sopwith said later: 'In the First World War we started by building aircraft without drawings, just sketches. I don't think anybody had the slightest idea as to how they were going to be developed in a comparatively short time.'

Expansion was rapid. The urgency of war set the pace.

The company's first important design was the Sopwith Pup, which commenced large-scale production in 1916. Able to maintain height in a dogfight – something few other aircraft could do at that time – it took the aviation world by storm. Then came the Camel, developed from the Pup. The two-gun Camel was hugely influential – later in the First World War, half of all fighter planes on the Western Front were Camels.

Just eight years had elapsed since Sopwith taught himself to fly. By age thirty, he headed the largest aircraft manufacturer in Britain. Yet after the First World War ended in 1918, everything changed. The immediate post-war years were a bad time for aircraft manufacturers. Sopwith Aviation struggled – and went into receivership. But in November 1920, with the support of Sopwith's loyal team, including Sigrist and Hawker, a new company was formed: H. G. Hawker Engineering Co.

Less than a year later, Harry Hawker was killed in July 1921 while flying a Nieuport Goshawk. He was just thirty-two years old. A shattering blow for Sopwith and the company, yet by the mid-1920s Hawker Engineering had received its first production contract for a new design, the Woodcock II, the first purpose-built night fighter to enter RAF service.

A twenty-nine-year-old draughtsman, Sydney Camm, had joined the company (see pages 30–3) and the later years of the 1920s saw an expansion of Hawker's as a manufacturer of military biplanes.

By July 1935, Sopwith stunned the aircraft industry and City institutions by setting up a trust to buy the Armstrong Siddeley Development Company, which embraced a number of large enterprises, including Gloster Aircraft, Armstrong Whitworth Aircraft, Air Service Training, and A. V. Roe (which would go on to produce the Avro Lancaster, the most successful British heavy bomber of the Second World War). These and other companies became Hawker Siddeley Aircraft. The original Hawker concern had evolved into an industrial empire.

By then, the British Government had begun to perceive the threat of war. Expansion of the British Navy, Army and RAF began. Within a couple of years, Hawker Siddeley Aircraft and its companies were fully engaged in mass-producing the planes that would go on to tackle the mighty German Luftwaffe. For the second time in his life, Tommy Sopwith ran a large aircraft-manufacturing concern during wartime.

By the end of the Second World War, the British aircraft industry had served the nation well. Many aviation firms had taken a crucial role. Hawker Siddeley Group had been responsible for Anson trainers (a plane used to train pilots), the Hurricane, the Typhoon and Tempest fighters, Armstrong Albemarle glider tugs, Whitley bombers, Lancaster heavy bombers, the Avro York transport and the Gloster Meteor – the first of the Allies' jet fighters. By then, the jet engine heralded a new aviation era; many jet fighter designs were developed, including another Sydney Camm masterpiece: the Hawker Hunter.

In 1953, Sopwith received a long-overdue knighthood. He retired as Chairman of Hawker Siddeley at the age of seventy-five, though retained a consultancy role for several years and actively continued with his many outdoor and country pursuits. He died in Hampshire in January 1989, aged a hundred and one – the last of the great aviation pioneers.

## 'HE WORE THE CROWN'

Sir Sydney Camm's passion for aviation design made him one of the world's greatest fighter-aircraft designers.

His background was humble. Born in a modest terrace house in Alma Road, Windsor, near London, in 1893, he was the eldest of twelve children. Their father, Frederick, was an artisan carpenter. As a child, Sydney developed a fascination for planes, working with his father to whittle propellors from wood. He left school in 1908 aged fourteen and was locally apprenticed as a carpenter and joiner.

In 1914, he joined the Martin and Handasyde Company based at the Brooklands racing circuit in Weybridge, Surrey (later to be one of the key sites of Hurricane production). Hired as a shop-floor carpenter, management spotted his talent and by the middle of the First World War, he was promoted into the company's drawing office, working mainly on biplane fighters. In 1923, he was selected by Tom Sopwith and Fred Sigrist to join the H. G. Hawker company as a senior designer/draughtsman. He was soon given significant responsibility.

The first design for which Camm was fully responsible was the Cygnet, a remarkable aeroplane with a variety of engines.

It won major light-aeroplane competitions in 1925 and 1926. Demand was growing for Hawker military aircraft, and when Camm became Chief Designer in 1925 his time was dedicated to military designs. During the 1930s he designed 84 per cent of the aircraft used by the RAF.

Sydney created fifty-two different aircraft types for Hawker. Those associated with him start with the classic Hawker biplanes – Heron, Hornbill, Hawfinch, Hart, Fury and all their variants – leading on to the arrival of the Hurricane, the Typhoon (with 56 Squadron in 1942), and the Hawker Sea Fury.

Following the huge advances of the jet engine after the Second World War, Camm designed the Hawker Hunter in 1951. In 1963 he was appointed Director of Design of Hawker Siddeley Aviation (Hawker Aircraft ceased in June 1963 and was formally subsumed into the Hawker Siddeley Group). Thereafter came Camm's contribution to a revolutionary project many years in development: the outstanding Harrier jump jet, the first-ever operational aircraft to deploy vertical take-off and landing (developed from the Hawker P1127).

History reveals Camm as the most influential aviation designer the country had ever known. Without this man's design of the Hurricane, the RAF would most likely have lost the Battle of Britain in the summer of 1940: at the time, there were not enough Spitfires emerging from the factories and out into the RAF squadrons.

Camm was knighted in 1953 and died in 1966. Those that knew him well said he was kind and courteous, a man of integrity and honesty, always surprised by the wide recognition of his successful designs.

Sixteen-year-old Graham Leggett worked as a Hawker apprentice in 1937 before joining the RAF as a Hurricane pilot. His personal description of Camm said it all: 'He wore the crown … In the world we lived in there was a lot at stake.'

Sydney Camm once summed up aircraft design in saying: 'The main requirements of an aircraft designer are knowledge of aerodynamics, some elementary maths and an eye for beauty.'

## EARLY HURRICANE DEVELOPMENT

The early Hurricane era goes back to 1933 when Sydney Camm and the Air Ministry started discussing the possibility of producing a fast single-seater fighter aircraft, based on Hawker's existing Fury biplane. The Fury had been designed by Camm and introduced in 1931, the first RAF operational fighter aircraft able to exceed 200 mph (322 km/h).

Relatively small numbers of the Fury were built – around 260 – and it remained with RAF Fighter Command until January 1939, though a small number were deployed in Europe and South Africa in the early years of the Second World War.

What remains most significant about the Fury is its design, with fabric skin, in a frame of metal tubes and wooden formers and stringers (attached frames). The skin was heavily painted with dope (a plasticized lacquer that was applied to fabric-covered aircraft) to reduce drag. Stressed metal wings were added later in development. Initially, it had a Rolls-Royce twelve-cylinder engine, later to become the Merlin engine. The outlines of the old Fury were readily discernible in the new Hurricane.

In 1933, the Air Ministry were not terribly keen on the idea of a fast monoplane fighter, despite the fact that a monoplane had already established a world speed record of 423 mph (681 km/h) in an Italian Macchi M.C. 72 in April 1933. As a result, government funding for the building of a prototype new monoplane fighter was not immediately forthcoming. Even in 1936, Britain's bomber and fighter squadrons would continue to rely on the older biplanes.

Nonetheless, Camm and Sopwith were already convinced of the future significance of a brand-new single-seater fighter. In a typically shrewd decision, Sopwith opted to proceed with the development of a prototype, funding the venture out of his own pocket.

With economy in view, the Hurricane was designed using as many existing tools and jigs as possible. Air Ministry funding for a full-size prototype finally came through in September 1934. Camm's design was of a cantilever monoplane, complete with retractable undercarriage and fitted with a Rolls-Royce Merlin engine.

There was, however, a crucial need for different thinking within the Air Ministry about the armament for fighters. Awareness was growing that in the development of high-speed fighter aircraft like the Hurricane, the traditional fire-power of two or four machine guns would not be adequate. Even a skilful pilot would not have time to get in a sufficiently destructive burst at the enemy. More guns would be needed.

There was stiff opposition to this idea at the Ministry. Some argued that the addition of more gun power might not be appropriate. A suggestion of eight guns was, to some, a staggering idea. Many felt these would weigh down the new planes – and it would be impossible to fit them on. These anxieties were set aside though in August 1934 when the Air Ministry ruled that 'eight guns should be aimed at on the grounds of shorter time to obtain the required density and the improvement in range which was obtainable with eight guns'.

Incredibly, it turned out that the key contribution to this very significant decision had emerged from an Air Ministry official – helped by his very bright teenage daughter.

## THE TEENAGE GIRL WHO HELPED WIN THE WAR

Captain Fred Hill was a scientific officer at the Air Ministry. A gunnery expert, he had helped develop gunsights and trialled new weapons for the Navy and Royal Flying Corps in the First World War. He studied the Air Ministry's specification for the new generation of fighter planes, analysed firing data and was strongly supportive of the belief that eight guns (rather than previous specifications citing two guns, then four) were now required for the new faster fighters.

So strongly did he believe this, he opted to enlist the help of his teenage daughter, Hazel – aged just thirteen – to prove his case. The maths involved was complex, with a great deal of data requiring analysis and research. He could take the research home, study it with his daughter, and, given Hazel's skill at maths, she could help him prove the argument for eight guns.

Armed with the latest calculating machines and gun-firing analysis, father and daughter worked through the night at home on the kitchen table in their north London terrace house. They plotted their way through the complex calculations. Examining speed, firing range and density of fire, these calculations showed that each plane needed to carry eight guns, carrying at least a thousand rounds a minute.

Fred Hill then used Hazel's calculations to create two graphs, which on 19 July 1934 were presented to the Air Ministry. They contributed to the decision that the contract with Hawker for the new Hurricane could be amended to include provision to carry eight guns, and work then commenced on incorporating this into the new Hurricane design.

Hill had told his superior officer at the Ministry, Claude Hilton Keith, of his daughter's help in the calculations – Hazel's contribution was even documented in Keith's memoirs, later published in 1946.

The eight-gun decision was incorporated into the specifications for the Spitfire. As a result, in June 1936 at the Hendon Air Show, young Hazel actually saw a new eight-gun Spitfire prototype. (Hawker's response to the need for an eight-gun fighter was the F36/34 Hurricane prototype.) As a thank-you for her work, Hazel was given permission to sit in the cockpit of the new plane.

'Four years later, in the Battle of Britain, eight guns were only just enough for us to win,' recalled Hazel's granddaughter, Felicity Baker. 'If we'd gone with four or even six, we would have most likely lost the battle … I remember her telling me she'd done the maths behind the guns. But I never really understood what that meant. She was really modest about it – in her eyes she had simply helped her father with mathematical calculations when he asked.'

Hazel Hill (1920–2010) went on to become a GP and later a child psychiatrist.

## FIRST FLIGHT OF THE HURRICANE

By August 1935, the various components for the new prototype fighter had been completed at the Hawker plant at Kingston. Then the completed sections were moved by road to nearby Brooklands for re-assembly in October 1935. Ground testing and taxi trials took place over the following two weeks.

Graham Leggett, then an apprentice at Hawker Aircraft,

witnessed the initial Hurricane construction process.

'At the initial construction stage it did not look all that different from all the biplanes we had been building, because the method of construction was almost identical, with steel tubes for the fuselage frame and high-tensile steel, which was rolled, for the wing spars and the tail-placed rudder main spars.

'On top of the steel tubular construction was placed the wooden framework, which was fairly lightweight. It was attached to the steel frame with nuts and bolts. It was only when we started putting on the stringers and the fabric that it began to look like another beast altogether. The fabric people would come with their great length of stuff and simply chuck it over the top. They were dress makers really.

'It would all be done by hand. The fabric would be pulled down into place and stitched together. When we put the thing up on stilts and put the undercarriage in with all the pumps and then filled it up with oil and started pumping the wheels up and down, this was an entirely new innovation. From that point onwards, it was a very different aeroplane.'

The 'very different' aeroplane flew as a prototype at the end of 1935.

On 6 November 1935, the first prototype Hawker Hurricane fighter, a small silver-painted monoplane, took to the air at Brooklands Aerodrome, Weybridge, Surrey.

The pilot was Flight Lieutenant (later Group Captain) P. W. S. George Bulman, CBE (1896–1963). He was Hawker's chief test pilot, described as a small, bald, ginger-moustached extrovert.

Bulman became a director of Hawker Aircraft later that year.

The prototype was developed in considerable secrecy. On that November day there were about eighty onlookers assembled, yet no press had been informed of this momentous event. Nor was any photography allowed. When the tarpaulins were removed and the hangar doors opened, there were a few murmurs of surprise. The plane – described at the time as the 'Interceptor Monoplane' – was bigger and heavier than any existing fighter, weighing in at more than 6,000 pounds (2,722 kg).

First impressions were good: Bulman reported that the aircraft flew comfortably and reached 300 mph (483 km/h) in a gentle dive with ease. Upon landing he was greeted by a jubilant Sopwith and Camm, who drove across the airfield in a Rolls-Royce.

Bulman did not file an official flight test report, opting to jot down his impressions on a notepad. He briefed Sydney Camm, commenting particularly about engine temperatures, which built up rapidly while taxiing. The temperature also increased quickly after the lowering of the wing flaps, suggesting that air flow was being retarded at the rear of the radiator. Bulman's major complaint was that the aircraft's canopy constantly creaked and flexed during the flight.

This first prototype carried a Merlin C No.11 engine, which was subsequently replaced by three different types of Merlin engine, until it was decided in September 1936 that production Hawker Hurricanes would carry a Rolls-Royce Merlin II engine. This alteration meant a slight redesign, which included tweaks to the plane's nose, propeller, air-intake engine cowlings, engine mounting, glycol tank and hand starting system, all of which led to the six-month production delay.

During successful further trials in early 1936 at the Aeroplane and Armament Establishment (owned by the Air Ministry) at Martlesham Heath, Suffolk, where testing and evaluation of many of the aircraft types flown in the Second World War took place, RAF test pilot Sammy Wroath (1909–95) said of the new Hawker Hurricane: 'The aircraft is simple and easy to fly and has no apparent vices.' (Wroath's test displays with the Hurricane quickly drew the attention of Hollywood's MGM studios, who requested that Wroath fly for them, standing in for Clark Gable in a 1938 movie, *Test Pilot*.)

In July 1936, the fighter was formally christened 'Hawker Hurricane' – a name that implied confidence and aggression – by the new monarch King Edward VIII during a visit to Martlesham Heath. (Hurricane itself was not entirely an original name since it had previously belonged to a short-lived Hawker plane of the 1920s.)

The maiden flight of the first production Hurricane, powered by a Merlin II engine, took place on 12 October 1937 at Brooklands Aerodrome, with Hawker test pilot Philip Lucas (1902–81) at the controls. Years later, Lucas revealed that once the faster speed of the new German fighters became known, there was a call to 'scrap' the Hurricane in favour of increased Spitfire production. 'Thank God we didn't!' he exclaimed.

Tommy Sopwith took a great interest in his test pilots, Bulman and Lucas. He would regularly visit them to see how the latest aircraft were progressing. Lucas – who was later awarded the George Medal for his skill and courage – also tested the Hawker Typhoon (introduced in 1941) and the Hawker Tempest (introduced in 1944).

The Hawker Hurricane swiftly drew much admiration. Between 25 November and 11 December 1938 at the prestigious Paris Air Show, some hundred thousand spectators from around the world viewed the latest aircraft. Massive crowds were able to examine the two new super-fast fighters, the Hurricane and the Spitfire. Few among them, of course, could have known they were watching the two British fighters destined to play such a hugely important role less than two years later in the Battle of Britain.

Hitler's superiority in the air was now firmly established: the Luftwaffe had at least twenty thousand airmen with operational experience from the Spanish Civil War. In just five years, Germany had become the best-equipped, most technologically advanced and battle-hardened air force in the world. For the British aviation authorities, this knowledge was daunting, to say the least. Britain was making inroads into catching up. Slowly. The Hurricane had finally entered RAF service, the first four of the new eight-gun Hurricane Mark Is having been delivered to No. 111 Squadron at RAF Northolt, just before Christmas in December 1937. In January 1938, twelve additional Hurricane Mark Is were delivered to No. 111 Squadron – the very first Hawker Hurricane squadron.

The speed – at 300 mph (483 km/h) – of the new fighters marked a huge turning point in aviation.

## 'THEY THOUGHT WE WERE WONDER BOYS'

Pilot Officer Ronald Brown (1914–2003) had joined the RAF as an aircraft apprentice in 1929 and received his wings at No. 111 Squadron at Northolt in 1937.

'In January 1938 we were equipped with Hurricanes – the first squadron to be equipped with monoplanes. On 18 January we were lined up and permitted to fly this aeroplane. We were not allowed to retract the undercarriage, we were not allowed to close the hood and we were told to do three circuits and landings. I did my three circuits. It was very noisy – because the hood was open and there was no top wing to keep the sun off your eyes. I thought it was quite an easy aeroplane to fly. Air Ministry, I think, were scared stiff that this aeroplane would get a reputation of being too fast for people.

'We were not allowed to do aerobatics until we had done fifty hours of flying with it, which was quite ridiculous, but having said that they did not want people pranging their planes all over the country. Anyone who did get it wrong left the squadron.

'The authorities were scared – and perhaps with good reason – that when they introduced the Hurricane – and a year or so later the Spitfire – that no one got the impression that the thing was difficult or dangerous.

'The media made an absolute meal of the Hurricane. We were wonder boys, specially chosen, travelling at these fast speeds, we got research information every day from the media, the staff colleges, to see these things in action.

'When I'd finished my first three circuits and landings I left the aeroplane with the brakes parked. An Australian pilot seconded to us took over from me. Off he went, leaving a great big skid mark down the airfield; he went round, did his circuit and did the shortest approach landing a Hurricane had ever done. He did his first circuit and landing with the brakes parked. Not long afterwards he landed in a plane with the wheels up! It wasn't until late 1938, I think, we fired our guns for the first time. And that was not a rush job.'

At the end of 1938, a total of 197 Hurricanes had been built.

A year later, the tally reached 731. By mid-1938, 50 Hawker Hurricanes had been delivered to RAF squadrons, including those delivered to RAF Kenley in March that year.

At Kenley, the aircraft needed every inch of the grass runways to get airborne. So much so, locals would hide in the bushes outside Kenley airfield to watch these 'modern marvels' only just manage to clear the hedges on take-off runs. On 5 May 1938, one of the new Hurricanes stalled on take-off and was badly damaged. Further deliveries to Squadron Numbers 56, 73 and 87 arrived in the summer of 1938, and later in the same year, 43 Squadron was re-equipped with Hurricanes.

The autumn of that year was to see the signing of the historic Munich Agreement – a precursor to the outbreak of the Second World War – ironically in the same city where Frank Murdoch had penned his urgent report to Sir Thomas Sopwith just over two years before.

## THE MUNICH FIASCO

On 30 September 1938, Britain's Prime Minister Neville Chamberlain returned to Heston Aerodrome after a meeting with Hitler in Munich. He was greeted by cameras – and cheering crowds. It looked like war had been averted. Millions in Britain, especially those who had experienced the tragic consequences of the First World War, were relieved.

Chamberlain waved a piece of paper, triumphantly claiming it demonstrated 'the desire of our two countries never to go to war with one another again'.

This 'Peace in our Time' headline was, of course, a false dawn. The 'no war for Britain' appeasement policy mistakenly hoped that British diplomacy could prevail to prevent war in Europe by ceding control of Czechoslovakia and the Sudetenland to Germany. It rested on Hitler's false 'promise' that his territorial aims, now so clearly in evidence, would stop there. They did not. So far as Hitler was concerned, promises were there to be broken. The Munich Agreement was a fiasco, described later by Winston Churchill as 'an unmitigated disaster'.

In March 1939, Hitler violated the Munich Agreement by occupying the rest of Czechoslovakia. Now it was obvious: Germany and Britain were preparing for war.


## HOW THE RAF EXPANDED

In 1934, the RAF had forty-two squadrons and some 800 aircraft. By 1939, this had grown to 157 squadrons and 3,700 aircraft. Alongside the increased aircraft production came an expansion of training to provide new air and ground crews.

The RAF Volunteer Reserve Force was launched in August 1936. It gave young men between eighteen and twenty-five the chance to learn to fly, free of cost, in their spare time. By spring 1939, there were 2,500 volunteer pilots in training, fully qualified by September of that year.

One such volunteer was Ray Holmes (1914–2005). When Ray signed up for the Volunteer Reserve aged twenty-two, he was a journalist working on the *Birkenhead Advertiser*, and was one of the earliest volunteers to join the Reserve in 1936.

'Flying became the be all and end all of life and time flashed by. Being able to write shorthand as a young reporter helped me to catch up with ground lectures. We all had large, stiff-backed notebooks, alternate-pages graph paper, labelled Form 620.

'Much of the work was straightforward. Engines I already understood, so learning about compression ratios, valve overlap, dry sumps, bonding and the like was no problem. On the practical side we learned to send and read Morse code by buzzer and lamp. The gunnery syllabus dealt with the Vickers.303 machine gun, firing 900 rounds a minute, which sounded an incredible rate of fire-power from an aircraft.

'I would have been dumbfounded had I known then that within four years I would be flying a Hurricane II in Russia with twelve Browning machine guns each shooting 2,400 rounds a minute or a total of 240 bullets per second.'

But if increased aircraft production was underway and new pilots undergoing training, would they fly fighters? Or bombers? How could the RAF achieve any kind of parity with the German bomber force?

For the time being, the emphasis had to be on air defence – doing everything possible to make a German land attack on Britain too difficult. Using the new fighters to help achieve this would require exploiting their much faster speeds, and the development of radio-based detection (known as radar). The threat was daunting, but as Churchill later put it so eloquently: 'we shall defend our island whatever the cost may be'.

There had been highly encouraging indications that the new Hurricane fighter would fulfil its initial promise. On 10 February 1938, Squadron Leader John Woodburn Gillan, Commanding Officer of 111 Squadron, flew a Hurricane 327 miles (526 km) from Northolt to Turnhouse near Edinburgh in under one hour. He took off just after lunch. But the weather worsened and to counteract a very strong headwind coming from the north he flew at full throttle (i.e. progressing as fast as possible) all the way.

He landed at Turnhouse around 4 p.m. and noted that the Hurricane's average speed had been 280 mph (450 km/h). The return flight was planned for the following day. But Gillan then decided that if he returned south immediately he would benefit from the strong tailwind.

He set off for Northolt once more in the gathering dusk, again at full throttle. Forced to fly higher than planned, he saw nothing through the clouds until, spotting the lights of Bedford, he eased the Hurricane into a shallow descent, breaking out of the cloud cover over north London. He touched down at Northolt just before 6 p.m., having completed the flight from Scotland in just forty-eight minutes at an average speed of 409 mph (658 km/h).

Gillan's flight introduced the Hurricane to the British public for the first time, bringing hugely enthusiastic newspaper headlines, and earning him the nickname 'Downwind Gillan'. The huge amount of publicity led to Gillan being immortalized in a cigarette card, his Hurricane L1555 becoming 'State Express 555' (the luxury cigarette brand's name) and Gillan being dubbed 'King of Speed'.

Wing Commander Gillan was killed in action in August 1941, while leading RAF 49 Squadron. He was shot down by an Me 109 while flying a Spitfire. His aircraft crashed into the English Channel and he was posthumously awarded a bar to his existing DFC (Distinguished Flying Cross). Afterwards, four Hurricanes were donated to the RAF by Gillan's mother, who had organized a 'John Bomber fund'. The name 'Our John' was painted on the cowling of one of the four, then named a

Hurri Bomber.

During the Hurricane's 'running in' period of 1938, as pilots gradually learned to handle the new advanced fighter, there were fatalities. The first death of a Hurricane pilot in peacetime occurred on 1 February 1938 when a Hurricane Mark I (L1556) flown by RAF Squadron 111's Pilot Flying Officer Mervyn Seymour Bocquet, aged twenty-two, crashed 'at a spinney on the edge of the Swakeleys estate'. The plane had dived into the ground at Uxbridge, Middlesex, one mile (1.5 km) west of Northolt. Bocquet had been promoted to Flying Officer less than six months before.

On 10 May 1938, No. 3 Squadron's Mark I Hurricane L1579 stalled on approach and crashed from about 200 feet (61 m) into the ground at Kenley, fatally injuring the young Pilot Officer Hugh Henry-May, aged twenty-one.

On 20 July, Squadron 111's Hurricane L1549 crashed at Hillingdon, Middlesex, while on approach to Northolt. Sergeant Maurice Reginald Kennedy-Smith was killed.

On 6 September, senior Hawker test pilot John Hindmarsh was killed after take-off. He had been testing a Hurricane at Brooklands Aerodrome. He had been advised not to fly above 10,000 feet (3,048 m) without oxygen. It is not known if he ignored this precaution, but the Hurricane, after wheeling high in the sky above Brooklands, was suddenly seen in a headlong dive. The plane struck the ground in an explosion at St George's Hill Golf Course, Weybridge. The contents of the fuel tanks exploded: Hindmarsh was killed on impact. Ironically, the crash was visible from the Brooklands track – where Hindmarsh, also an accomplished motor racing car driver (he won the Le Mans 24 Hour Race in 1935) had driven many of his greatest races.

Despite such tragedies, the pace of building the new fighters was accelerating. By September 1939, 497 Hurricanes were in service with seventeen squadrons, including No. 3 Squadron, which had reverted to the Hurricane in May 1939.

Quantity increased and quality improved. It was decided to enlarge the rudder and incorporate an underfin after sixty-one planes had been built and spin issues investigated by the RAF. Better radios and exhausts were fitted. The old two-bladed wooden propellers – which could break into pieces under stress and were inefficient – were replaced by a de Havilland metal three-bladed two-pitch propeller. This improved fuel economy and rate of climb.

Other improvements followed. Armour plate and bullet-proof windscreens offered more protection for the pilot. Metal wings replaced fabric-covered ones. Not every Hurricane was fully converted by the outbreak of war in September 1939 – even in August 1940 there were still a few in service with the old fabric-covered wings or wooden propellers – but most had been.

From 1938 to 1940 the Hurricane also began its role as an exported fighter. Significant numbers were sold overseas. Many of these would eventually play an important role in the Second World War.

The Hurricane export drive was aimed initially at Yugoslavia. Hawker Aircraft had already developed a relationship with the country in the 1930s. In December 1938, twelve Hurricanes were flown to Yugoslavia, via France and Italy. Twelve more were delivered in February 1940. In November 1938, twelve Hurricanes had been purchased by Romania (delivered just days before the German invasion of Poland on 1 September), and in the winter of 1938/39 seven Hurricanes were shipped to South Africa. These formed No. 1 Squadron SAAF, creating considerable excitement when flying from Durban to Pretoria at 335 mph (539 km/h). In April 1939, twenty Hurricanes were ordered by the Belgian Government, and a licence to build another eighty was given to leading Belgian aircraft manufacturer Avions Fairey. Turkey ordered fifteen Hurricanes, delivered from Brooklands in September 1939. Persia (now Iran) purchased eighteen, only one of which arrived in Tehran before the Second World War broke out.

The Polish Government purchased one Hurricane for evaluation: Poland's air force liked the plane so much that nine more were ordered for the summer of 1939. On 1 September 1939, the Nazis invaded Poland, so further deliveries had to be diverted to Gibraltar. Nonetheless, the Polish flyers' initial experience in combat against the Luftwaffe would prove important in the near future, many of them going on to fight in the Battle of Britain (see Chapter 3).

## WHY THE EXPORT DRIVE MATTERED

By the late 1930s, the RAF urgently required new planes. Why, then, were significant numbers of Hurricanes being exported at a time when war was on the horizon?

On 6 May 1939, journalist William Conor wrote in the *Daily Mirror*:

> The Hurricane is one of the finest fighter machines in the world. Less than four months ago, the Secretary of State said that we needed between five and six thousand fighter planes for home defence. We haven't got them yet or anything approaching it. So what is the answer to selling Hurricanes to Yugoslavia when we desperately need every machine here?

The answer was not immediately obvious. Yet aside from

Tommy Sopwith's need to generate additional income for Hawker Aircraft, there were other important factors:

- The heavy pre-war financial burden on the British Government. This meant the Treasury was desperate for foreign currency earnings, given the threat of the looming war.
- Some of the initial foreign orders would most likely generate a further increase in Hurricane production.
- Selling the fighters to countries then described as the Dominions (or the British Empire) made sense. They were already linked closely as allies of Britain. The mostly pro-government newspaper, *The Times*, defended the sale of Hurricanes to South Africa thus: 'The Hurricane is a much faster type of aircraft than anything in regular use in the South African Force. It is desirable that pilots of the Union shall have some training in the types of aircraft which will have to be acquired in the event of war, and the first batch of Hurricanes will be used to that end.'

The outcome of Hawker's export drive overseas would indeed prove hugely important. These countries and their airmen would go on to play a crucial role in the history of the Second World War.

## CANADA'S HURRICANE QUEEN

In the autumn of 1938, the Canadian Government ordered twenty Hurricanes. The first of these went into service in February 1939. In turn, this helped set up a deal with the Canadian Department of National Defence, so that Hurricanes for the RAF could be manufactured in Ontario by the Canadian Car and Foundry Company. In total, 1,451 Hurricanes were built in Canada.

A key figure in this Canadian success story was Elsie MacGill (1905–80), Chief Designer at Canadian Car and Foundry. MacGill was a pioneer of aeronautical engineering, remarkable not just because of her gender – she was the first woman in Canada to receive a bachelor's degree in electrical engineering and the world's first woman to earn an aeronautical engineering degree – but doubly so due to her triumph over disability.

After completing her master's degree in aeronautical engineering in 1929, she contracted polio, a contagious viral disease that can cause paralysis, breathing problems and death. (Only from the 1950s and 1960s did vaccines bring the disease under control.) At first, it looked like Elsie would spend the rest of her life in a wheelchair. Undaunted, she succeeded in learning to walk again, helped by two metal canes. Once mobile, she began her engineering career at Fairchild Aircraft in Quebec, joining Canadian Car and Foundry in 1938. Overseeing the Canadian Hurricane production, she even designed a winter version, with skis and a de-icing facility, another aeronautical first. The Hurricane contract to produce aircraft in Canada ended in 1943. But such was her success that, thereafter, she would always be known as the Queen of the Hurricanes.

There was an additional factor in outsourcing some of the production of the Hawker Hurricane: a fear of Luftwaffe attacks on aircraft factories. Those fears accelerated as, on 1 September, Germany invaded Poland from the west. Two days later, France and Britain declared war on Germany. At 11.15 a.m. on Sunday 3 September 1939, Prime Minister Neville Chamberlain made a historic BBC broadcast. Hitler had failed to respond to British demands to leave Poland.

'This country is at war with Germany.'

Eight minutes later, air raid sirens were sounded in London, sending people hurrying to the shelters. But nothing happened. It was a false alarm. Yet the prospect of terror from the skies or a potential invasion by the enemy was now all too real. Those who had spent years producing warplanes like the Hurricane – and those men already trained to fly them – well understood that it was no longer 'the eleventh hour'. Conflict lay ahead ...

# CHAPTER 2

# IN THE AIR

## FRANCE, SEPTEMBER 1939

### 'WE'RE READY'

IN SEPTEMBER 1939, POLAND, NORWAY, DENMARK, Belgium, the Netherlands and France were about to experience, one by one, the might of Hitler's blitzkrieg, or 'lightning war'. Within less than a year, these countries would fall, defeated by the swift, focused tactics of Nazi Germany.

So much lay ahead. Yet in that momentous 3 September broadcast to the nation by Prime Minister Neville Chamberlain, Britain and France were jointly declaring war on Germany. Only the English Channel – and the pilots of the RAF – protected Britain from a huge Nazi invasion.

The Hawker Hurricane had reached the first stage of war: the RAF now had nineteen fully equipped Hurricane squadrons across the country. Four of these squadrons, Nos 1, 73, 85 and 87, were already preparing to defend France. It had been agreed that short-range tactical bombers and fighter aircraft from Britain would move to French airfields, supporting the French forces on the Western Front.

The French initially demanded ten RAF squadrons. Britain's response was to refuse: the government believed that the French air force was not sufficiently well organized. Ten became four squadrons, along with the regiments forming part of the BEF (British Expeditionary Force).

Mobilization of the BEF (army, navy and air) started as soon as war was declared. Troops from the British Army and Territorial Army were deployed to Europe to take up strategic positions along the Franco-Belgian border. Troops, vehicles and material were sent there over the next six months: by March 1940, the BEF consisted of over three hundred thousand men.

The French believed their key military defence against Germany was the Maginot Line, a concrete fortification system running through France along its border with Germany. Their confidence would be shattered. The German Army would conquer France by invading through the dense forests of the Ardennes, bypassing the Maginot Line. Mechanized forces, i.e. tanks, heavily supported from the air by the Luftwaffe, could get the Germans across the difficult, rough terrain.

Before war had broken out, the German Luftwaffe had been practising attacks on shipping or ports, while Hurricane squadrons took part in air exercises around south-east England. The prevailing mood in Britain was 'We're ready.'

Harold Bird-Wilson (1919–2000) was based at Croydon with No. 17 Squadron, newly equipped with Hurricanes in June 1939. Once war was declared, he recalled:

'There was a general feeling, let's get on with it. There was no fear or anything like that. We felt we had one of the best aircraft in the world, the Hawker Hurricane, and we could take on the Germans. There was no worry in the squadron as regards casualties. We did not think much about the superiority of the Luftwaffe. We thought we could present them with a good fight.'

The months between September 1939 and April 1940, when very little fighting actually occurred after the invasion of Poland, are frequently described as the Phoney War. That gap in time from winter to spring gave both sides breathing space in which to prepare their land and air forces for the approaching onslaught. The period was not entirely without incident though. On the very same day that war was declared, the civilian passenger liner, SS *Athenia*, became the first British ship to be sunk by Germany in the Second World War, torpedoed by submarine U-30 off the coast of Ireland.

Eventually, it was France that would witness the very early days of the Hurricane in combat. Hurricane Squadrons 85 and 97 took up their base at the airfield of Boos, near Rouen, in the north-east of the country. No. 73 Squadron had its base further west at Rouvres in north-central France. Squadron No. 1 was based at Vassincourt airfield near the north-west border with Belgium. The Hurricanes were assigned to protect the Advanced Air Striking Force (AASF), a group of Bristol Blenheim and Fairey Battle light bombers deployed to mount attacks and carry out reconnaissance across the Maginot Line.

No. 1 Squadron was the leading fighter squadron of the day – it had received its first Hurricane Mark Is in October 1938. Based at Tangmere, West Sussex, it was also the very first RAF Fighter Squadron to be deployed to France.

RAF Tangmere has a long proud history along England's

south coast. In the years between the two World Wars it had boasted one of the RAF's finest fighter squadrons. Located near the Roman town of Chichester, between the South Downs and Selsey Bill on the English Channel, Tangmere's airfield had been enlarged in the late 1930s to defend the coast against attack by the Luftwaffe.

Even today, a springtime walk in the countryside around the village of Tangmere hints at a bucolic setting, an English idyll.

In March 1939, twenty-two-year-old Paul Richey (see pages 58–60) was posted there. Paul's summer at Tangmere had passed in a flurry of anticipation.

'Half the pilots of each squadron now had to be permanently available in case of a German attack. Our days were now spent in our Hurricanes at air drill, air firing, practising battle formations and attacks, dogfighting – operating under ground control with the new super-secret RDF (Range and Direction Finding – what we now know as radar, then a 'revolutionary' new technology of radio-based detection and tracking).

'The standard of flying in 1 Squadron was red hot. The squadron proceeded to demonstrate that the Hurricane could be easily and safely performing aerobatics in formation and below 5,000 feet [1,524 m].'

Pilots were, however, still finding their way with the new fighter.

'One dived down a searchlight beam at night and hit the Downs at 400 miles an hour [644 km/h]. And I vividly remember, half an hour before I took a Hurricane up for the first time, seeing a sergeant pilot coming in for a forced landing with a cut engine. He was too slow on the final turn and spun into the ground on the edge of the airfield.'

Richey was the first to reach him.

'He had been flown clear but blood was running out of his ears and he was dying. However, fatal accidents were a fact of flying life and 1 Squadron's peacetime average of one per month was considered normal.'

At one stage, Richey's squadron were visited by Squadron Leader Coop, British assistant air attaché in Berlin. He gave the pilots a lecture on the Luftwaffe. Stark news. The Luftwaffe had over 3,500 aircraft, including 1,300 bombers and 380 dive-bombers. Even with the confidence in the Hurricane's abilities, Britain could not possibly match that.

'We were staggered by the number of superbly equipped German bomber and fighter squadrons. These figures rammed home what a narrow escape England had had at the time of Munich and as that glorious last summer of 1939 rolled on it became clear it was no longer a question of whether there would be a war, but merely when it would come. In August we learned we would soon be leaving for France.

'Shortly afterwards one of our hangars was stacked with transport and mobile equipment to take with us. We heard that several RAF Fairey Battle squadrons had already left and we would be off at any moment. We also heard that Air Marshal 'Stuffy' Dowding, Commander in Chief of Fighter Aircraft, was kicking up a stink with the Air Ministry: Dowding strongly objected to surrendering the four fighter squadrons to go to France with the BEF.

'He even paid us the compliment of stating that he would not hold himself responsible for the defence of London if we were sent abroad.'

Tangmere became the designated stopping-off point for all squadrons moving across the Channel to support the British Expeditionary Force.

On the first night of war, No. 1 Squadron was called to readiness at dusk. Nothing happened. Just an uneventful hour in the air and a call to return.

The next few days proved equally uneventful: that first week of war at Tangmere remained tense with anticipation. When would the Germans start their attack?

'There was no more news of our impending departure for France. Our time was spent standing by our Hurricanes and scrambling at each alarm.

'We expected to be bombed at any minute, but no bombers came and the tension gave way to a feeling of unreality.'

Finally, on the morning of 8 September, No. 1 Squadron was called to make ready for France.

'We were soon grouped beside our Hurricanes. We ripped the squadron badges from our overalls (by order) and I gave mine to a fitter. We jumped into our cockpits. We took off in sections of three, joining up into flights of six in sections-astern, then went into aircraft line-astern.

'Down to Beachy Head for a last look at the cliffs of England, then we turned out across the sea. Not a cloud in the sky, scarcely a breath of wind on the sea and the heat in the cockpit was almost unbearable, as we had on all our gear — full uniform, overalls, web equipment, revolver, gas mask and Mae West [the inflatable life jacket]. Only the almost complete absence of shipping in the Channel brought home to us the fact that there must be a war on somewhere.

'After about thirty minutes Dieppe appeared through the heat haze and we turned down the coast towards Le Havre. Our airfield at Havre lay north-west of the town on the edge of 400-foot [120-m] cliffs. It was new and spacious with an unfinished hangar on one side. On the other side, surrounded by trees, was a long low building that turned out to be a convent commandeered to billet us. The squadron closed in, broke up into flights of six, then sections of three, and after appropriately saluting the town, came in to land individually. We taxied to a welcome from our troops. No. 1 Squadron had arrived in France, the first British fighter squadron to do so.'

On 30 October, No. 1 Squadron claimed the Hurricane's first victory in the war. Pilot Officer Peter 'Boy' Mould shot down a Dornier Do 17 over Vassincourt. Afterwards, Paul Richey wrote an account of the combat in his diary.

'Having seen the Dornier, Mould took off without waiting for orders, pulled his plug [boost override], lost the Hun, climbed to 18,000 feet [5,486 m] — and found him.

'He did an extraordinary straight stern attack, firing one longish burst with his sights starting above the

Dornier and moving slowly round the fuselage. The Hun caught fire immediately, went into a vertical dive and made a whopping hole in the French countryside. It exploded on striking the ground.'

There were no survivors. The mangled remains of a gun from the aircraft together with a bullet-pierced oxygen bottle later adorned the squadron mess: trophies of the first British fighter victory of the war.

'Five hands were all that remained of the crew of four, but four coffins were given a funeral with military honours at which the squadron was represented. We were all pleased with our first success but we were sorry for the poor devils we had killed.'

"Boy" got very drunk that night and confided in me: "I'm bloody sorry I went and looked at the wreck. What gets me down is the thought that I did it."'

## PAUL RICHEY

Paul Richey was born in London in 1916. His father, Lieutenant Colonel George Richey, fought in the trenches in France in the First World War. His mother was Australian. Educated in Switzerland and England, he was commissioned by the RAF in May 1937 to train as a fighter pilot.

At twenty-four, he was already a veteran of aerial combat, an extraordinary hero. He shot down six German planes in a series of No. 1 Squadron patrols in the initial campaign in northern France between March and May 1940, returning to his squadron base at Vassincourt in his Hawker Hurricane each time. On 11 May he was shot down. He managed to bail out but suffered concussion. He returned to operational flying as soon as possible.

His last patrol of the Phoney War came on 19 May after downing his third Heinkel He 111 bomber. Richey was hit by a burst of fire from a bomber's rear gunner. He managed to crash-land in a field in Amiens with a serious bullet wound to the neck. He spent a month recovering in a Paris hospital. On returning to England, he discovered he'd been awarded a DFC and Bar.

Paul Richey went on to write a remarkable book, *Fighter Pilot*, chronicling his months as a fighter pilot in the Battle of France. The book, the first-ever account of aerial combat written by an RAF fighter pilot, was published anonymously in 1941 to great acclaim. In the spring of 1941, after the publication of the book, he returned to operational flying, joining 609 Squadron as senior flight commander of Spitfire Vbs at Biggin Hill.

Like many Hurricane pilots who were later flying Spitfires, he was initially apprehensive about the change. He knew little about the Spit – and had seldom even seen one.

'I also had the Hurricane's conversion: I never hoped to fly a better fighter. This was perhaps understandable, for although an older machine than the Spit, the Hurricane had been well tried in peacetime. It had done magnificently in the Battle of France [and later Battle of Britain] and had shot down far more enemy aircraft than the Spitfire.

'My own battles had been fought on the Hurricane, I had every confidence in it and I was thoroughly at home in one.'

And so he approached the Spitfire

> 'with a certain amount of distaste. On the ground, to my
> biased eye, the Spit looked knock-kneed, flimsy and rather
> silly. It lacked the robust strength of my beloved Hurri'.

After he'd flown three circuits and landings and some mild aerobatics, he taxied in, 'feeling worried and disappointed, wondering whether it was the plane or me that was wrong'.

His brother-in-law Micky was there to meet him.

'How'd you like it?' he said with a smile.

'Not much,' I said glumly.

'Don't worry, old boy,' he said. 'I felt the same after I'd come off Hurricanes but after I'd done about twenty hours I wouldn't change it for anything. You'll see.'

Later Richey commanded 74 Squadron and in May 1942 he returned to 609 Squadron on Typhoon Is at Duxford. Following postings as Wing Commander to the Far East and India, having suffered from severe sinusitis at one stage, he was invalided home in February 1944. Following some time in hospital he took up a post in SHAEF (Supreme Headquarters Allied Expeditionary Force) before ending the war at HQ RAF 2nd Technical Air Force.

For a short post-war period he worked for the *Daily Express* as air correspondent, then later for BP. He was also awarded the Belgian and French Croix de Guerre.

He died in 1989, aged seventy-two.

## THE STORY OF 'KILLER' KAIN

On 8 November 1939, a few days after No. 1 Squadron's first wartime victory, a young New Zealander, Edgar 'Cobber' Kain, out on reconnaissance patrol with 73 Squadron, shot down a Dornier Do 17 in a daring combat manoeuvre. In the following year, 'Cobber' (the name is an Australian and New Zealand word for 'mate') proved to be one of the most brilliant fighter pilots of the early part of the Second World War.

He was the very first RAF Ace (an aviator credited with shooting down five or more enemy aircraft) and the first RAF fighter pilot to be awarded the DFC during the war. He was also the RAF's very first celebrity fighter pilot, his name and image being splashed across the pages of newspapers in Britain and France – and around the world.

Almost every story from war correspondents in Britain and France contained accounts of Kain's successes. At one stage he was more written about in the French press than in Britain. The French loved him.

'He was a very flamboyant aviator, very determined and confident,' recalled his 73 Squadron comrade Dickie Martin. 'A splendid extrovert, an excellent pilot and a good shot with a very good eye.'

Kain (known to family and friends as 'Eddie') was born in 1918 in Hawkes Bay, New Zealand. He took flying lessons in New Zealand and applied to the RAF for a short service commission in 1936, travelling to England for training at his own expense. After training he was posted to 73 Squadron. He went to France with them not long after war began.

Following that first confirmed kill on 8 November, his Hurricane was shot up and caught fire during an engagement on 23 November. His parachute was not properly attached, so he made an emergency landing at Metz. He suffered burns – then continued to fly.

On 26 March 1940, he shot down a Messerschmitt Bf 109, the backbone of the Luftwaffe's fighter force. On that occasion his Hurricane was severely shot up and shell fragments wounded his leg. He managed to bail out.

Between 10 May and 20 May he shot down five more enemy aircraft, then a Dornier Do 17 bomber on 25 May. Again his Hurricane was damaged and he made a crash-landing. The following day, 26 May, he downed a high-wing Henschel Hs 126 – and another Dornier Do 17.

His celebrity as a heroic young fighter grew with every success. In April 1940, readers learned that the 6-foot-tall (1.8 m) dark-haired New Zealander was engaged to a beautiful twenty-three-year-old actress named Joyce Philips. They had been sweethearts since 1936, when Kain was training with the RAF. They planned to marry in July 1940.

One Paris-based English correspondent who knew the young airman well was journalist Noel Monks.

'There was some quality in the whimsical boy from far-off New Zealand that endeared him to everyone who came in contact with him, not only as a great destroyer but as a natural, friendly, unspoilt young man.

'No one ever heard Cobber Kain brag. No one ever knew him to go about with his chin stuck out, looking for trouble. Out of the cockpit of his fighting machine he was mild mannered and peace loving. In the cockpit he was a killer.

'He became France's first hero of the war. Several times when I was on leave in Paris with him he was mobbed by French people, male and female, old and young in the Champs-Élysées or in the foyer of a theatre. "Monsieur Cobbaire" they called him.'

On 31 May, the streets of Paris were crowded with people wanting to cheer the young hero.

'It was the last time I was ever to see him and he had never looked fitter and neater. He had on a brand-new uniform, his hair was cut, his eyes were clear. He looked just what he was: an officer and a gentleman. When we parted that night, Cobber said: "Don't put it in the paper but I'm getting married next week. That is, if I'm alive."'

But by then the 'Phoney War' in the air had ended. The German Army had now crashed through the Ardennes – and were rapidly advancing further into France. RAF squadrons in France initially retreated to different airfields.

On 5 June, Kain shot down a Bf 109. The following day he was stood down. RAF operations in France were about to end. He would be returning to England.

On the morning of Friday 7 June, he climbed into his Hurricane at his squadron base at Échemines airfield, south-east of Paris. He planned to fly to Le Mans, pick up his kit and then fly back to England. In three weeks' time, he would celebrate his twenty-second birthday and marry his fiancée.

As a last salute to his squadron, he opted to carry out some low-flying aerobatics only just above their heads (a manoeuvre known to pilots as a 'beat up'). His Hurricane climbed, he kicked it into a turn, roared down low and did a barrel roll over the airfield. Gaining height and turning, he came back in the other direction and did another at 200 feet (61 m), travelling at over 300 miles an hour (483 km/h).

Then, his Hurricane swooped in low as he began another roll, but the wing-tip of the Hurricane touched the ground ever so slightly – just enough to cause the aircraft to cartwheel and crash onto the runway. The Hurricane exploded on impact.

Kain was hurled 90 feet (27 m) away. Injuries from the crash killed the young New Zealander.

A day before Cobber's last flight, he'd been in Paris briefly. Stood down, he shared a drink in a café with Paul Richey. Richey remembered their conversation.

> 'He was on a few hours' leave. Cobber told me the rest of the original 73 Squadron had gone back to England and that the squadron had been re-formed. He had stayed behind to help get things going. He said they'd had some losses — five killed and several wounded, I think. I noticed that he was nervous and preoccupied and kept breaking matches savagely in one hand while he glowered into the middle distance.
>
> 'Like the rest of us, he'd had enough for a while.'

In his brief life as a Hurricane Ace, Cobber Kain notched up an incredible total of seventeen confirmed 'kills' of enemy aircraft. His Hurricane Mark I, L1826 was the last 73 Squadron Hurricane still fitted with its original two-blade fixed-pitch wooden propeller.

Cobber was buried in north-eastern France at the Choloy Allied War Cemetery. His headstone reads: 'Cobber Kain, you inspired our little nation. New Zealand remembers. Adieu.'

## THE KILLER WASP

If Paul Richey and Cobber Kain were among the most widely celebrated Hurricane pilots in 1940, they were not the exception.

Pilot Officer Arthur 'Taffy' Clowes (1912–49) was another immensely skilful aviator. He had joined the RAF in 1929 as a seventeen-year-old aircraft apprentice, later qualifying as a metal rigger. After pilot training he, like Richey, flew with No. 1 Squadron at Tangmere at the outbreak of war.

On 23 November 1939, a Heinkel 111 was heading home when it was spotted at 20,000 feet (6,096 m) between Verdun and Metz by three Hurricanes from No. 1 Squadron. They chased it over the German frontier. They attacked it repeatedly – but their guns were frozen (due to the altitude). The bursts that finally brought the Heinkel down were from Taffy Clowes.

As he broke away, six French Morane Saulnier (M. S.406, the first modern fighter aircraft to be adopted by the French air force) rushed in. One smashed into Clowes's tail. It destroyed part of the rudder and one elevator. The French pilot bailed out. Somehow, Clowes managed to get his Hurricane back to Vassincourt, only to crash-land on arrival. As he emerged from the cockpit, Paul Richey noted: 'he was laughing – and trembling violently'.

On 29 March 1940, a trio of No. 1 Squadron pilots, Johnny Walker, Bill Stratton and Taffy Clowes, destroyed three Me 110s while on patrol over Metz at 25,000 feet (7,620 m). A dogfight ensued at 2,000 feet (610 m). Walker and Stratton ran out of ammunition and returned to Vassincourt. Clowes, however, disposed of two Me 110s. His Hurricane had out-manoeuvred them.

Clowes was promoted to Flight Sergeant on 1 April 1940. That same month a newly delivered Hurricane Mark I, P3395, became his personal aircraft. In August 1940 he was awarded a DFM (Distinguished Flying Medal) for his courage in France that spring.

Determined and humorous, Clowes opted to paint a fearsome-looking wasp motif on either side of the new Hurri's nose, underneath the exhaust stubs. His plan was to add a further painted black stripe onto the 'wasp' each time he shot down enemy aircraft in his Hurri. One stripe equalled one 'kill'. His final score totalled twelve.

In May 1941, Clowes was awarded a DFC. He commanded 79 Squadron from December 1941 to February 1942 and 601 Squadron in the Western Desert from August to November 1942. In May 1943, he took command of 94 Squadron at the Egyptian fortress of El Gamil. But that autumn he had to relinquish his command. He had been accidentally blinded in one eye. When war ended he remained with the RAF, as a staff officer at their Staff College.

Sadly, he died in December 1949, aged thirty-seven, at the RAF Hospital in Ely, Cambridge. He had developed liver cancer.

## FIRST IMPRESSIONS OF THE HURRI

The three Hurricane flyers above had demonstrated extreme courage and skill in one of Britain's earliest battles with the enemy. But what of the hundreds of newly trained young Hurricane pilots? They had benefited from those months of relative calm in the Phoney War, because they had provided an eventful learning curve.

Pilot Officer Donald 'Dimsie' Stones (1921–2002) was one such young man. He'd joined 32 Fighter Squadron at Biggin Hill in January 1940. No. 32 Squadron had recently converted to flying early Mark I Hurricanes, which had replaced the Gloster Gladiator biplanes.

During his training at St Athan, South Wales, the month before, Dimsie learned to fly the Hurricane, an exciting prospect for an eighteen-year-old.

'I had seen the Hawker Hurricane going through its Air Ministry trials at Martlesham Heath. I knew roughly its dimensions and that it was powered by a Rolls-Royce Merlin engine of more than 1,000 horsepower, but most of its details then were still on the "secret list". Now I was actually going to fly one.'

On 29 December 1939, a line of Hurricanes and Harvards were drawn up outside the St Athan hangars. Dimsie Stones was ready to learn, reporting to Flight Lieutenant 'Pan' Cox, who knew the Hurricane well. Cox escorted Stones on a tour of inspection.

'We started at the de Havilland variable-pitch three-bladed airscrew. He explained its operation from fine to coarse pitch, obtained by the varying angle of attack of its blades. Then we examined the massive V12 cylinder Merlin engine. As it was liquid cooled, there was a coolant tank which contained glycol, much more efficient than water.

'The massive radiator for the coolant hung below the engine between the undercarriage bays. Airflow through the radiator was controlled by adjusting a wide shutter or flap at the rear of its housing using a lever situated in the cockpit.

'We progressed around the Hurricane noting the four gun-ports closely positioned in each wing. These were kept covered by fabric "gun" patches until they were blown off by the .303 ammunition when the guns were fired. As they were replaced after each sortie [mission], you could always tell if a pilot had been in combat when he landed and taxied into dispersal, by looking at the patches.'

Then came the young man's magic moment of climbing into the port wing-root via the retractable foot stirrup and getting into the cockpit, sitting on the parachute already resting in its bucket seat.

'My first impression was that it was bigger than I expected. It was much larger than the Harvard's, it was very similar to the cockpit of the old Hawker Audax biplane which I'd flown in.

'Every aircraft has its own smell. To me, all Hurricanes smelt of rubber and some sort of disinfectant containing alcohol, which I always put down to the glycol coolant, not — please God — to petrol leaking from the 45 gallons of 100-octane petrol in the reserve tank situated immediately in front of the pilot, just behind the engine.

'I tried the flying controls by moving the "stick" and they responded smoothly, ailerons rising to meet the stick when it was moved towards them. The ailerons rising with the stick eased back and vice versa. The rudder moved similarly but sideways as the pedals were pushed to one side or the other.

'I could not find the brakes until Pan showed me the hand lever incorporated in the circle of the stick's head. It was exactly like the brake lever on a bicycle. It applied air pressure to the wheel selected by means of the rudder pedal, thus controlling the direction of the aircraft while taxiing on the ground.

'Pan told me to make frequent checks of the air pressure gauges between my feet, as not only the brakes were operated by air pressure but also the guns.

'I went through the motions of lowering and raising my

seat, opening and closing the radiator flap – important because the great Merlin engine heated quickly on the ground – it should be closed gradually to stabilize the coolant temperature when airborne. Opening and closing the cockpit canopy with one's left hand was also important because one's right hand would be on the stick when flying; so opening the cockpit for landing, which was a strict rule, must be done with the left hand.

'If you want to jump out in a hurry to use your parachute,' [Pan told him], 'you want to do it smoothly and quickly, so always see it's not jamming before you take off.'

Now it was time to start up the Hurricane, following Pan's instructions.

'After starting up, let the coolant temperature warm up to that mark and your oil pressure and temperature at those,' he said, pointing at the gauges. 'Run up the engine, check both your magneto ignition switches, throttle back a bit and check your airscrew pitch lever into coarse and fine, note the drop in revs when you are in coarse and don't forget to put it back into fine for take-off or you won't get off the ground. Do all the checks on the pre-flight check card.

'Don't forget that when you are running up the engine to full revs with the stick fully back you have your ground crew lying on your tail plane to keep the tail down. So don't suddenly take off with him still on the tail; he doesn't want a free flight as the poor bugger hasn't got a parachute. Don't forget that when you are taxiing the Hurricane around the grass, SWING THAT

BLOODY GREAT NOSE in front of you to see where you
are going.'

After following his instructions, Dimsie waved away the
chocks, checking that he did not have a passenger on his tail.

'I saw what Pan meant about the enormous nose ahead
of me. Nothing could be seen directly ahead unless one
used the brakes and rudder pedals to swing it from side
to side.'

Lined up on the take-off run with a green light from the control
tower and a crackling message in his earphones, he gradually
opened up the 1,030 horsepower Merlin engine to full throttle,
keeping her straight with the rudder.

'Stick slightly forward and the tail came up. Then we
were airborne. I selected wheels up and eased back
the throttle to climbing power. Noticing that the nose
pitched up and down more than I expected, I soon got
used to it and smoothed it out.'

The pre-take-off butterflies had gone, replaced by tremendous
exhilaration.

'I was flying the Hawker Hurricane, the RAF's main fighter,
and I could feel the power of it in my hands, feet and
backside. I made a long and careful approach for my
first landing, bounced a bit and then turned round for a
couple more circuits and landings.'

Dimsie's training ended on 24 January 1940. He'd been assessed above average. Then he learned he was joining 32 Squadron at Biggin Hill.

> 'My cup brimmed over with delight. I was to join the elite.'

## A MEETING WITH CHURCHILL

Dimsie had just returned from a cold, uneventful patrol in March 1940 and was warming up by the fire in the mess when he heard the station commander, Wing Commander Dickie Grice, saying: 'I expect you'd like to meet some of the pilots, sir.'

> 'We recognized the unmistakable figure of Winston Churchill, bow-tie, cigar and all. He was First Lord of the Admiralty then.
>
> '"Sit down gentlemen," he said, lowering himself onto the upholstered fender around the fire. It dawned on us he lived nearby at Chartwell and this was probably just a neighbourly visit.
>
> 'I was sent to rustle up the mess staff to bring tea and anchovy toast. When I returned he was holding forth on his view of the war so far. He was already holding a glass of something better than tea.
>
> 'One of my flight commanders was asking could Churchill give them any idea when the war would really get started?
>
> 'Churchill looked thoughtfully at his glass and then at us.
>
> '"I can only think that the Boche is waiting for fine

weather. Otherwise he would come through us and the French like a hot knife through butter.'"

Churchill – who on 10 May stepped in as Prime Minister after Neville Chamberlain's resignation – was right. By then, Germany had invaded Denmark and already embarked on a full-scale invasion of Norway on 9 April. Denmark had capitulated. On the very day Churchill became Prime Minister, Germany invaded France and the Low Countries, i.e. Holland, Belgium and Luxembourg; a few days later, it bombed Rotterdam and the Dutch Army capitulated.

Eighteen Hurricanes were sent off to help stem the German invasion of Norway. No. 46 Squadron Hurricanes were put aboard the aircraft carrier HMS *Glorious* by crane. Despite this vessel not being equipped for carrier operations, the take-off proved no problem, as the engineers of HMS *Glorious* achieved 30 knots, giving the Hurricanes sufficient wind over the deck to get airborne safely.

Along with Gloster Gladiators of 263 Squadron, the Hurricane provided patrols over the port of Narvik. Fierce combat against daily raids led to some fourteen German aircraft being shot down. But faced with the German advance, the squadrons were ordered to evacuate on 7 June. The remaining eight Hurricanes and ten Gladiators flew back to HMS *Glorious*, landing safely on the same day.

On 8 June, HMS *Glorious* and two escorting destroyers encountered gunfire from German battleships and all three were sunk – with a loss of over one and a half thousand officers and men. On board were the Hurricanes of 46 Squadron. It was the worst blow suffered by the Royal Navy since the start of the war. Only two of the Hurricane pilots survived.

It had long been understood that the BEF was seriously ill

equipped to fight the Luftwaffe in France. The Bristol Blenheims, Fairey Battles and Lysanders had proved no match in combat – they were mostly too vulnerable and unsuited to the demands of modern aerial warfare. Hurricane squadrons based in France had been increased, but there were nowhere near enough fighters or Allied bombers to make a difference to counter the devastating impact of the Me 109s. Moreover, the French Moranes and Dewoitines could not possibly deter the Messerschmitts. In the air and on the ground, the battle for France was rapidly being lost.

Group Captain Dennis David, CBE, DFC and Bar, AFC (1918–2000) had joined 87 Squadron and first flown to France on 9 September 1939. By May 1940 the Hurricane crews knew that the Battle of France had turned into a nightmare of constant danger, soaring losses and draining fatigue. Said David:

> 'To give you an idea of the numbers we were up against, six of us ran into forty Ju 87s dive-bombing a hospital. We shot down fourteen of them and on our way back to our base, having dispersed the raid, I saw another 150 going on the same target. It was not a feeling of loss but a feeling of helplessness. How can you cope with those numbers?'

By the end of June 1940, David was awarded the DFC with Bar – and credited with eleven enemy aircraft destroyed.

There was another issue. Experience in the air also made a huge difference to the enemy. The German fighter units had already fought in Spain and Poland. Yet the Hurricane squadrons – like 607 – had only recently been converted from Gladiators, with just four weeks' training with the Hurricane.

'Few, if any of our pilots had sufficient experience on type to be classed as "operational", recalled 607 Squadron's Peter Parrott, whose image, taken in early March 1940 by a photographer accompanying a group of war correspondents, was later used in the RAF's first-ever recruitment poster.

By mid-May 1940, the German advance had broken through on the borders of France and Belgium at Sedan. At that point, the RAF was experiencing the worst day it had endured throughout the Battle of France: twenty-seven Hurricanes shot down, mostly by Me 109s. Seventeen pilots were killed.

On 15 May, as the Netherlands fell to the German advance, Squadron Leader Thomas Gilbert Pace (nicknamed 'Ace' Pace) of 85 Squadron flew alongside two other squadron pilot officers in his Hurricane Mark I N2656 as the trio attacked a group of fifteen Heinkel 111s south of Ath, Belgium.

Pace's first day of action in France had taken place just five days before – after his posting to 85 Squadron on 26 April. The young man set one enemy plane on fire, then he too was attacked, possibly by a Messerschmitt Bf 110 escort, firing 20-mm cannon shells. He managed to crash-land in a field, but he was severely burned when the forward fuel tank behind his instrument panel exploded, showering his thigh with burning fuel. Somehow, he succeeded in throwing himself out of the burning cockpit and rolled on the ground to extinguish the fire. Then he walked half a mile (0.8 km) until meeting an army motorcyclist, who summoned an ambulance.

Here is part of a letter he wrote in November 1940 to Miss Peggy McFarlane of Montreal. At the time he was recovering at Park Prewitt Hospital, Basingstoke, from severe burns to his hands and face.

*I got one bloke beautifully in the sights and gave him the works. He was just beginning to smoke nicely when something hit me eight times, an awful smash. One of their Heinkels had been potting at me, so I had to try and shoot him, but the engine was faltering badly and then thick black smoke started pouring from under the dashboard. Mixed with it, all acrid, was the smell of glycol. I had my main oil pipe cut and a couple of 20-mm shells in the radiator. Then there were two more bangs and the wireless disappeared.*

*I thought that the best thing to do was to force land and save the machine, or at least some of it. I couldn't see any flames so I never thought of using my parachute. I could just see through the Perspex on the left-hand side, and during my various coughs and splutters, I picked a field. Just crossing the boundary, I hit a tree with my right wing. I couldn't see it owing to the smoke. There was a terrific crash, then I ducked inside the cockpit. As I hit the ground there was another crash and a sound of rending metal and a slithering sound. Then there was a terrific pop and the whole thing was a mass of flame. The sliding hood, which I had so carefully opened, shut and jammed, the gravity tank below the dashboard exploded and spilt burning petrol on my right thigh. I tried to open the hood but couldn't. The temperature was getting a bit warm and I tried again and I succeeded in getting it open a little. I remember telling myself to keep cool; seems funny, doesn't it? I heaved at the hood and it came open enough for me to get out halfway. Then my parachute caught on the seat and I hiked myself out and landed on my right shoulder in the port petrol tank, which was burning beautifully. I picked myself up after rolling off the wing onto the ground. How I did it I don't know, but I walked half a mile and then came across an army motorcycle.*

The letter had been written after he'd already spent several months at Prewett Hospital. At the time of writing he had undergone four major operations. Sir Archibald McIndoe, the New Zealand-born renowned plastic surgeon, had worked on him (see Chapter 3).

Pace very much wanted to return to flying and had been told he could do so after a final operation. In the letter he said he planned to get his sportscar (nicknamed The Mousetrap) to the hospital when he left – it would save him money on bus and taxi fares.

Once recovered, he returned to operational flying. On 3 December 1941 he flew Hurricane I AF985 from RAF Silloth in Cumbria. The station was used by RAF Coastal Command. It is not known what happened because both Pace and his aircraft were designated lost without trace.

He is commemorated at the Air Forces Memorial to the Missing at Runnymede, Surrey.

## 'WE NEED MORE HURRICANES'

On 15 May 1940, Winston Churchill received an agonized phone call from the French Prime Minister Paul Reynard saying, 'We have been defeated, we are beaten, we have lost the battle.' In the weeks prior to that phone call, many in France seemed to be clinging fervently to the notion that, despite its perilous position, the country might somehow be saved with the help of more British Hurricanes. There was a sadly mistaken belief that the powerful Hurri could somehow physically stop the German tanks.

Of course, it was a wholly fanciful notion– it would be two years before a tank-busting version of the Hurri saw action.

Churchill knew all too well that sending more Hurricanes at a time when Britain was also facing attack was a seriously risky proposition.

A compromise was reached. Six additional Hurricane squadrons would be sent over from England to France at dawn, thus enabling them to return to English stations at dusk. This was a politically expedient move – it underlined the superb reputation the Hurricane fighter had already built up – but it was a fruitless gesture, nothing more.

At Biggin Hill, 32 Squadron was one of the six Hurricane squadrons to be sent over to France during the daytime, returning to England at night.

Pete Brothers (1917–2008), who was to become one of the RAF's most outstanding fighter pilots, remembered the confusion of the nigh-pointless arrangement to support France.

'We would take off from Biggin Hill half an hour before first light, land at primitive French bases during the day, then get back to Biggin after dark.

'Communications were appalling and we could not get instructions from anyone. We could not make contact with the air headquarters to find out what they wanted us to do. We were having to refuel our own planes from jerry cans and to start them ourselves.

'We were starting these Hurricanes with handles, which meant I would get into my aircraft and two of the chaps would wind the handles and start it and we would then leave it idling. I would get out and help start his. So it went along until we had got all twelve going.

'It was a scene of general chaos.'

Along the roads, the French were now fleeing in desperate retreat. The German Luftwaffe was deliberately attacking civilian groups to create panic. This blocked the roads and completely disrupted Allied communications.

History records a tragically painful sight: crowds of refugees pushing prams, handcarts and in some cases horse-drawn carts; women carrying babies, and toddlers clutching their mothers' hands – all of them fearful of more attacks from the air. There were few cars. Dogs and horses were left on the roadside, mostly dead or half dead.

The RAF paid dearly during those final weeks of the Battle of France. Its total losses from 10 May to 22 June were 931 aircraft and 1,526 casualties. Four hundred and seventy-seven fighters were lost over France and the Channel – 386 of them were Hurricanes. Many abandoned Hurris had to be set on fire because there were no spares, meaning it was impossible to repair them. A fifth of the trained pilots were dead or disabled. Back in Britain, half the remaining pilots were newly trained and without experience.

On 20 May, in the face of the German advance, the Air Ministry ordered the withdrawal of the remaining Hurricane squadrons. Squadrons 1, 73 and 501 remained to the south of Paris, finally departing around 17/19 June.

One young Sergeant Pilot with 501 Squadron had only recently joined them as they were about to withdraw from France. James 'Ginger' Harry Lacey (1917–89) joined the RAF Volunteer Reserve in 1937 as a trainee pilot. After war broke out, he joined 501 Squadron prior to its move to Bétheniville in those final weeks in France. He was about to experience battle for the first time.

On 13 May, in his first-ever combat, he destroyed a Heinkel He 110 over Sedan. On 27 May, he claimed two more – just before the squadron withdrew from France on 19 June.

Later, he said that he would rather fly in a Spitfire – but fight in a sturdy Hurricane. The Hurricane, he said, 'was made of non-essential parts. I had them all shot off at one time or another and it still flew just as well without them.'

Lacey was typical of many Hurri pilots. There are innumerable stories of men landing in Hurricanes with little idea anything was wrong – until they saw the faces of their 'erks' (the ground crew).

## DUNKIRK: WHERE WERE THE HURRICANES?

By mid-May 1940, Winston Churchill had ordered preparations for ships and vessels to evacuate British and French forces from the French coast. Fresh troops were rushed from England to defend Boulogne and Calais, but by 26 May both towns had fallen to the Germans. The small port and seaside town of Dunkirk was the only remaining location from which to evacuate the forces.

The story of what happened next is already well documented. From 26 May to 4 June the evacuation, named Operation Dynamo, involved the rescue of 338,000 British and French soldiers from the beaches of Dunkirk. Organized by the Royal Navy, it provided a huge boost to civilian morale in Britain. Yet for many years after the event, there was confusion surrounding the lack of airborne assistance to the BEF rescue at Dunkirk. Where were the planes?

The RAF had sent all available aircraft to protect the evacuation – but by then, their resources were severely stretched.

Between 26 May and 3 June, a total of fourteen Hurricane units operating from British bases were involved in the evacuation – and were later credited with 108 air victories.

Twenty-seven Hurricane pilots became flying Aces during Operation Dynamo. Many of these were Canadians from Squadron 242. Losses were twenty-two pilots killed and three captured.

But the reality was that any aircraft sent to protect those trapped on the Dunkirk beaches were at the mercy of the Luftwaffe as wave after wave of German dive-bombing Stukas, Messerschmitts and Heinkel He 111 bombers came at them.

Furthermore, the one-hour flight from England to the French coast was close to the fighters' operational limit, giving them too short a time over the combat area to be effective. And at that time, there was no radar to warn them or ground control to guide them. They were also facing anti-aircraft fire from both German and British batteries. British destroyers at Dunkirk were desperately firing at anything and everything in range.

Squadron Leader Norman Hancock (1920–2008), then a pilot officer with No. 1 Squadron, recalled the aerial confusion over Dunkirk.

'You went as a squadron towards your target. You were in appropriate formation but once you'd engaged the enemy, by and large people tended to split up and individually attacked targets. You didn't stay as a solid machine of twelve aeroplanes pointed in the right direction. It didn't work that way.'

On 18 June, the last of the Hurricanes on the continent were finally recalled to Britain. Of the 452 Hurricanes sent to battle in France, just 66 returned. Almost all the units' ground equipment was lost there. Fifty-six pilots had been killed, 18 were now prisoners of war and 36 had been wounded. The

Luftwaffe had lost 1,428 aircraft in battle – the majority of these attributed to the Hurricane.

On that same day, after the German swastika had been raised over Paris, just four days before the French would formally surrender, Winston Churchill addressed the House of Commons.

> 'The Battle of France is over ... the Battle of Britain is about to begin. Upon this battle depends the survival of Christian civilization. Upon it depends our own British life, and the long continuity of our institutions and our Empire. The whole fury and might of the enemy must very soon be turned on us. Hitler knows that he will have to break us in this island or lose the war ...
>
> 'Let us therefore brace ourselves to our duty and so bear ourselves that, if the British Empire and its Commonwealth last for a thousand years, men will still say: "This was their finest hour."'

Just three weeks later, on 10 July 1940, the German Luftwaffe began bombing Britain.

The Battle of Britain had started ... and the Hurricane was about to fly into the very epicentre of the story ...

# CHAPTER 3

# THE BATTLE AHEAD

## 10 JULY-31 OCTOBER 1940

THE BATTLE OF BRITAIN PROVED TO be the Hawker Hurricane's greatest and most memorable success in the air. This should never be underestimated, since by the summer of 1940 Germany had already demonstrated its huge air power. France had been overrun and Germany now held most of north-west Europe.

As Paul Richey pointed out, even with its confidence in the Hurricane's abilities, Britain could not possibly match Germany's air power.

Outwardly, Britain appeared to be greatly disadvantaged. It seemed that the Luftwaffe held the advantage in the air, and would be able to fight their way across the Channel, destroy the RAF – and invade Britain.

In fact, German resources were not infinite – their own losses in the air had already had an impact by then.

Consider the numbers. By 9 August 1940, just before the launch of the full air offensive by Germany, British air forces, operating day and night fighters under Fighter Command, had 60 operational squadrons with a total of 715 serviceable aircraft ready for operation. These were not as far short of existing German total aircraft as might have been believed at the time. German aircraft operational forces on 10 August totalled 1,011 aircraft with 805 fighters immediately ready to fly.

These numbers would change considerably, of course, following the German offensive. Yet aside from that, Britain had one unique advantage during the Battle of Britain: Fighter Command's system of integrated communication and intelligence gathering.

## THE DOWDING SYSTEM

The Dowding system was a ground-controlled interception network controlling the airspace across Britain from Scotland to the south coast of England. It had been developed by Fighter Command's Commander in Chief, Air Chief Marshal Hugh Dowding.

Socially awkward, sometimes garrulous or aloof, Dowding was nicknamed 'Stuffy'. His career was drawing to its close by the time of the Battle of Britain. But it was Hugh Dowding who understood the significance of Britain's ground-controlled network of defences, including its radar stations (also known as Chain Home stations), and the technical issues and organizational skills involved in running these.

Radar, though still in its infancy, was capable of detecting and locating incoming enemy aircraft heading across the English Channel. By early 1940, thirty coastal Chain Home radar stations had been constructed. These ranged from Cornwall to the far north of Scotland, with half of them built along England's eastern and southern coasts directly facing the enemy. Eleven of the most important radar stations had 'shadow' stations a few miles distant. There were also thirty-one Chain Home Low stations built – these were aimed at detecting aircraft flying under 1,000 feet (305 m).

Radar was far from perfect. So it was supplemented by additional information from the Royal Observer Corps.

The Royal Observer Corps consisted of around thirty thousand men and women volunteers who had trained themselves in aircraft recognition, so that they could keep watch on the skies from around a thousand posts across the country. These observers, who used binoculars and the Post Instrument (the standard optical sighting system to determine the location of aircraft), could ascertain the size and height of the enemy formations making their way across the Channel.

This information concerning incoming raids was fed (by dedicated phone lines set up at the radar posts) to the central operations room, Fighter Command's HQ (or Filter Room) based at Bentley Priory, located in Stanmore, north-west London. Here the estimated numbers, speed and altitude of approaching aircraft could be 'plotted' using very large maps. The process of feeding the information directly to HQ's Filter Room could take as little as four minutes, just enough time for fighter aircraft to be airborne. In this way, Britain's limited numbers of aircraft could then be positioned to best advantage – and at short notice.

Britain was not alone in using radar – in fact, it had been invented in Germany. But the Germans, at that all-important turning point of July 1940, did not quite understand the role played by Britain's radar and its use within Dowding's communications system. They assumed that British radar was not very sophisticated – as a consequence, it got less bombing attention than might have been expected.

The Germans also assumed that RAF fighters were tied closely to the area around their station and did not possess the crucial information the Dowding system gave the RAF. They also misunderstood the RAF's capacity to reinforce with men and aircraft. Well into 1941, they wrongly assumed that the RAF could not replace its losses fully.

The British, on the other hand, overestimated the size and range of the German air force and assumed the Germans had greater numbers of pilots – which was never the case. They also mistakenly believed that the German bombers and long-range fighters could cover the whole of the British Isles from French bases and that the German short-range bombers could reach as far as Hull – when in reality, the Germans could barely contest air space over London.

These contrasts in perceptions turned out to be hugely significant.

By then the Hawker Hurricane was already increasing Britain's air power. From June 1940 onwards, nearly one and a half thousand more Hurricanes were manufactured. (Spitfire production lagged behind Hurricane output until early 1941.)

The Hurricane Mark II, which began to arrive in June 1940, had a higher rate of climb – but it was slightly slower, 354 mph (570 km/h) against 362 mph (583 km/h) at 18,000 feet (5,486 m). Small deliveries were made of the Mark IIA, which had a maximum speed of 342 mph (550 km/h). Both marks had a ceiling of 34,000–35,000 feet (10,363–10,668 m).

By the end of the Battle of Britain, the RAF had two hundred more Hurricanes at operational readiness.

When you look back at Sopwith's canny pre-war decision to

start building a thousand Hawker Hurricane fighters without a firm government order, that decision was more than fully vindicated by late 1940.

It wasn't luck. It was shrewd foresight.

## WHO WERE THE 3,000 MEN WHO FLEW IN THE BATTLE OF BRITAIN?

There is a stereotypical idea – which for some reason has endured down the decades – that a typical RAF fighter pilot was a British upper-class man with a handlebar moustache and a highly privileged background.

The reality of wartime changed everything. In the event, the men who flew the Battle of Britain aircraft came from across the globe, flying alongside established British RAF pilots. The battle was a truly international victory. Many were from what were then little-known countries in Europe. By July 1940, sixteen nationalities of young fighter pilots from overrun European countries had already made their way to Britain after the fall of France, offering their services to the RAF and its squadrons.

By then, thanks to the Battle of France, many experienced British pilots had been killed, wounded or were, quite simply, exhausted, resulting in an urgent need of fully trained fighter pilots for the RAF. In the summer of 1940, the training system had to be overhauled – to bring in three RAF operational training units.

Trained pilots from France, Belgium, Poland, Czechoslovakia and Norway were more than ready to fight. Yet there was initial hesitation from the RAF – due to the difference in language, for instance – though its view soon became much more accommodating.

Polish pilots had already fought desperately – in ancient fighters – to protect their homeland, making their way subsequently via Hungary and Romania to France, where they volunteered to fight again. Then, when France fell, they volunteered to fight in England.

A total of a 145 Poles, 88 Czechoslovaks, 29 Belgians, 13 Frenchmen and an Austrian flew in the Battle of Britain. Alongside these were the flyers from what were then known as Commonwealth countries: 126 New Zealanders, 98 Canadians, 35 Australians and 25 South Africans flying alongside 3 Rhodesians, a Jamaican, a Barbadian and a Newfoundlander.

Ten Irish and eight US pilots also fought, even though their countries were technically neutral at the time.

In a matter of weeks, the skill and courage of these men defending the cause of civilization would prove to be awe inspiring.

The largest foreign contingents in the Battle of Britain were the Polish pilots. Their contribution and skills became the stuff of legend. Despite having been operational for just six weeks, the Polish 303 Squadron went on to claim 126 victories in the battle – the top-scoring RAF unit.

Four national fighter squadrons – Nos 310 and 312 (Czechoslovak); Nos 302 and 303 (Polish) were formed – all equipped with Hurricanes.

The skill and dedication of these men in the air was backed up, round the clock, by an equally committed ground crew, whose contribution involving the repair or fast turnaround of the Hurricane also merits huge recognition. Ground crew comprised fitters, riggers, armourers, drivers, cooks and storemen, among other trades, all pulling together as a team to keep the aircraft serviceable for pilots ready to scramble at a moment's notice. These men shared in the successes and the losses, with little recognition of their role, yet all were happy to know they were 'doing their bit'.

Following German raids, the ground crew would tow damaged aircraft away from runways to make room for others to land, repair damage elsewhere, fight fires, and help pilots out of aircraft – sometimes while under fire themselves. Many were killed. Throughout the war the RAF recruited and trained thousands of pilots and ground crews from Caribbean, Indian and African countries.

Joe Roddis (1922–2017) was an engine fitter for the RAF throughout the Battle of Britain and for the rest of the Second World War, serving first with 234 Squadron and later with 485 NZ Squadron. He worked on Hurricanes and Spitfires, and over the post-war years maintained a good relationship with some of the veteran pilots he'd worked with, sharing the triumphs and the losses that affected ground crews in equal measure.

'If it was your own pilot, of course it affected you. If not, you were still sorry – a mother had lost a beloved son.

'It was teamwork, certainly; sometimes you weren't all happy jacks; but in general, it worked well. As far as pilots were concerned, we were on the ground making sure they could fly – but only the pilots could do what the plane was meant to do. I'd never call an officer anything other than "sir" as a mark of respect for what they did.'

The pilots' behaviour after hours, was, at times, quite extraordinary.

'On one occasion, three pilots came back with a Buick which they'd stolen. Then the police turned up.'

Sometimes pilots would let off steam in ways that wouldn't have been tolerated in peacetime: one, for example, used to tie two cats' tails together and douse them with petrol – as entertainment.

'It was terrible. But you knew how much strain they were under.'

The Battle of Britain had distinct phases:

- 10 July–7 August: German attacks on coastal shipping, some limited attacks on radar installations and airfields in southern England.
- 8–23 August: Intensive attacks on radar installations and southern England airfields.
- 23–24 August to 6 September: Continuous attacks on aircraft and aircraft factories.
- 7–30 September: A switch – Luftwaffe attacks on London.
- 5–31 October: Daylight attacks discontinued in favour of massive night attacks, as well as nuisance daytime raids by Bf 109 fighters.

## THE HURRI FITTER'S STORY

Eighteen-year-old Eric Marsden trained as an engine fitter with 83 Squadron in 1939. In May 1940, he was sent to 145 (Hurricane) Squadron at Tangmere. The squadron had recently converted to Hurricanes.

By then, the Hurricane Mark I had undergone modifications. Fabric-covered wings had been replaced by re-stressed material-covered wings. An armour-glass panel had been incorporated on the front of the windscreen and the 'rod' aerial mast replaced by a streamlined, tapered design. From May 1940, 70 pounds (32 kg) of armour-plate protection had been added as head and back armour.

Within ten days of Eric Marsden's arrival at Tangmere, events in France and the Low Countries had created such pressure on fighter defences that 145 Squadron was declared operational and began patrolling over the BEF, or rather beyond them, trying to cut down the number of enemy aircraft strafing the retreating forces.

For a while pilots were able to land at forward landing grounds at the end of the first sortie of the day, returning to Tangmere in the evening, after a day of up to six or seven sorties against or in search of enemy aircraft.

'On arriving back at Tangmere, our pilots were dog tired and tended to crawl into bed straight after debriefing. The following morning, we got stuck in immediately to servicing the kites, working as long as necessary on repairs where needed. Badly shot-up kites were taken out of service and the flight's spare kites brought into use whenever we had them.

'It was a matter of pride to have the maximum number of serviceable aircraft. Bad unserviceability reflected badly on everyone in the squadron. As the retreat continued, forward landing grounds were lost and the squadron began operating from RAF Manston in Kent during the day, supported by a forward servicing party.

'With the completion of the evacuation from Dunkirk

there was a short lull during which time "Boydy" [Flight Lieutenant Adrian Hope Boyd] began to sharpen us up in the business of what became known as a "scramble" – getting sections of aircraft held at "readiness" into the air as quickly as possible.

'We began to live with one of three states: "readiness", "standby" [with a time attached from immediate standby to fifteen or thirty minutes] and "released" [stood down]

'At "readiness" everyone was on tenterhooks, waiting for the signal for furious activity. In the other two states we were to work like blazes on any unserviceable aircraft. Only when the kites were in the air could we sit still. The loudspeaker above the pilot's crew-room door allowed us to hear the R/T [radio] between our own squadron pilots in the air, sometimes distressing when you heard someone you like in deep trouble.

'Boydy came to the conclusion that a scramble should be achieved within two minutes of receiving the phone call at dispersal.

'This was impossible to achieve when the pilots had their parachutes clipped to their posteriors. It was also quickly established that the kites should be started up by the ground crew but this meant sitting for hours in an aluminium bucket seat with the front edge biting into the underside of the thighs, awaiting a signal from a large electric bell fitted outside the crew-room door, to start our machines.

'Not until the parachute was kept in the aircraft's bucket seat, with all the harness straps laid out over the cockpit edge, so that the pilot could be strapped into the kite, with the engine warm and running, could we achieve the two minutes or less, with teamwork by the mechanic and rigger.

'Despite the different trades, most pairs would take turns in the cockpit, the second member sitting on the starter trolley by the starboard wing-tip, ready to press the button on the "trolley-acc" on the signal from the person in the cockpit, who would then press the starter button to spin the engine.

'Immediately the engine fired up, the other person on the "trolley-acc" would run to the nose of the kite, by the leading edge of the wing, to unplug the heavy starter-duty starter cable – a screwdriver job, often in a worn-out slot. After retrieving the cable and pulling the heavy "trolley-acc" clear of the kite, he would then run to the trailing edge of the starboard wing to reach into the open bay of the fuselage behind the pilot and turn on the oxygen supply, replacing and fastening the fairing panel while suffering the blast of the prop.

'From there he ran to the starboard side and front of the kite to be in view of the pilot, until the mechanic, who had been strapping the pilot in place, had jumped down to the port and front of the kite to await the "chocks-away" signal from the pilot.

'It was somewhere about the end of June that we received orders to repaint the underside of our kites in the new "sky" colour, specified as a mixture of so many parts matt white, so many parts an unremembered blue and so many parts yellow, with the aim of producing a somewhat duck-egg blue.

'However, stores played their usual part, not enough of the right blue, not enough of the right yellow, so we had to use what we could get.

'In addition we were painting aircraft which were black on one wing, white on the other. This, together with the fact that the paint was being mixed in limited quantities, resulted in a flight line where the kites varied in colour from a strongish light blue to a distinct duck-egg green, and mostly with a darker port wing, where the black showed through. Some of the kites coming in as replacements from the maintenance and repair units had been painted over the old black and silver underside scheme and showed different again. It was quite a long time before we achieved anything like a uniformity of colour.

'June and July were marked by a continuous flying effort, a steady drain on our original set of pilots and the introduction of the Rotol 35-degree variable-pitch, constant-speed propeller and two technical sources of controversy: a new harmonizing arrangement [so that the Hurricane's guns were aligned such that bullet streams would converge at around 400 yards (366 m), though by the summer of 1940, harmonization at a range of 250 yards (229 m) became standard] and the 'Big Wing Theory' [a massed formation of fighters intended to intimidate the enemy].

'The Jablo-bladed Rotol props were regarded as the best thing since sliced bread, giving better climb and better engine control. As to the harmonizing, we saw our drivers and armourers with the pattern boards for the new and old systems.

'To most of us ground crew the patterns on both appeared to be irregular, random arrangements so that we wondered what was the purpose of these curious scatters of aiming points.'

The "Big Wing" idea cut right across Boydy's thoughts on the right way to tackle the interception problem.'

## THE BIG WING STRATEGY

The Big Wing strategy involved up to five squadrons of fighter aircraft flying together in one large formation, allowing them to meet the incoming enemy in strength.

It was a controversial tactic as far as the politics of those at the top were concerned. When the daylight bombings petered out (7 September–5 October) the tactic emerged. It was inspired by the legendary Wing Commander Douglas Bader, whose Duxford squadrons (based in East Anglia and Lincolnshire) flew out of Duxford that September in these large formations of fighters five times. In October, there were ten Duxford Big Wing missions – shooting down one enemy plane. 'Big Wing' had not been a success.

By late July and early August 1940, the tempo of the air war had steadily increased. Recalled Marsden:

> 'Our pilots were getting distinctly frayed around the edges and I know that one or two considered themselves as "written off" already – it didn't affect their attitude to flying and fighting but they had no hope of survival for themselves.
>
> 'It was a grievous time for us, for we could do little to help. We couldn't take their places, though most of us would have given anything for the chance.
>
> 'It might not be incorrect to say that our respect and liking for our pilots almost became love at this time – and we had to watch them, indeed help them to take

off to go and die in ones and twos, until the core of battle-trained men became dangerously small.

'We had "good" days like the one on which the squadron claimed, I think, twenty-one victories, eleven going to our flight. Whatever may have happened as a result of analysis of records and claims and consequent adjustment of scores, our blokes honestly thought they'd knocked down that many and we were credited with them and given a day's rest by no less than Sir Archibald Sinclair himself [Secretary of State for Air] who came down to see us, accompanied by a news film unit who took shots of wholly unreal "squadron scrambles", all aircraft in neat vics [three or more aircraft flying in close formation with the leader at the apex] all nice and tidy.

'It was nothing like the chaos of the real thing, when the kites belted off straight from their dispersal point, regardless of wind direction and formed up in the air.'

On 14 August, 145 Squadron was moved to Drem, near Edinburgh, Scotland. After the war, Eric Marsden lived in Hampshire and became a history teacher.

## THE YOUNG FIGHTER PILOT'S STORY

Tom Neil (1920–2018) joined the RAF as a Reserve at the age of eighteen and was called up to full-time service at the outbreak of the Second World War. As a pilot officer he was posted to 249 Squadron in May 1940. He flew Hurricanes from RAF North Weald in Epping Forest, Essex, during the Battle of Britain, flying 141 times against the Luftwaffe and

ABOVE: The original Battle of Britain survivor and combat veteran, the Hawker Hurricane Mark I R4118 was delivered new to 605 Squadron on 17 August 1940. During the Battle of Britain, it flew forty-nine sorties and shot down five enemy aircraft. It is seen here being flown by pilot James Brown over Duxford Airfield, Cambridgeshire.

LEFT: Peeling away, this shot is reminiscent of a Hawker Hurricane heading into battle. The Hurricane was more durable than the more celebrated Spitfire, which made it popular with pilots and ground crews alike.

ABOVE: Sir Sydney Camm (seated), aeronautical designer, studying a design of the Hurricane at his Thames Ditton home in 1941.

ABOVE RIGHT: Sir Sydney Camm seen here at Byfleet, 1915. His favourite hobby was making model aircraft and thrilling his young sons with stories of his inventions.

RIGHT: Australian aviation pioneer Harry George Hawker at Hendon Aerodrome, *c.* 1920.

LEFT: Women's Auxilary Air Force (WAAF) armourers and flight mechanics servicing a Royal Air Force Hawker Hurricane at Sealand, Flintshire, Wales, May 1943.

BELOW: Wren air mechanics feeding ammunition into the Browning gun of a Hawker Hurricane aircraft.

LEFT: WAAF armourer trainees, cleaning and assembling the Browning guns of a Hawker Hurricane fighter.

RIGHT: A woman welding a fuel tank for a Hawker Hurricane fighter airplane at Fort William, Ontario, Canada. 1941.

LEFT: The Hawker Hurricane production line at The Hawker factory in Langley, c.1941.

BELOW: The first production Hawker Hurricane Mark I monoplane fighters with the two-blade fixed pitch wooden propeller of No. 111 Squadron Royal Air Force Fighter Command, c. July 1938, at RAF Northolt, London.

CENTRE: The Hawker Hurricane IIC, PZ865, The Last of the Many, the final production Hurricane is rolled out of the Langley factory in 1944

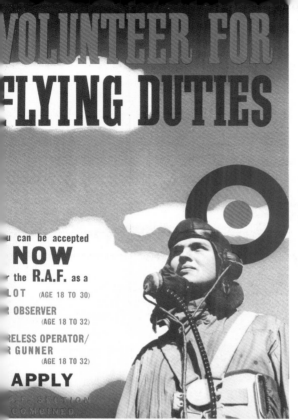

Text visible on poster:

VOLUNTEER FOR
FLYING DUTIES

u can be accepted
**NOW**
r the **R.A.F.** as a
...OT (AGE 18 TO 30)
R OBSERVER
(AGE 18 TO 32)
RELESS OPERATOR/
R GUNNER
(AGE 18 TO 32)
**APPLY**

LEFT: A recruitment poster featuring RAF pilot Peter Parrott.

BELOW: Prospective Royal Air Force recruit Michael Suthers arrives at Euston Combined Recruits Centre and is attracted by a poster showing a formation of Hawker Hurricane fighters in flight, November 1940.

Text visible on poster:

MIGHTIER YET!

Every day more PLANES
Every day more PILOTS

LEFT: Pilots and officer standing with a row of 111 Squadron Royal Airforce RAF Hawker Hurricane Mark I parked behind.

BELOW: Squadron Leader (later Group Captain) Peter Townsend With ground crew at his Hawker Hurricane in Wick, Scotland 1940.

ABOVE: Pilots of No. 85 Squadron RAF pause for a photograph between sorties at Lille-Seclin, at 9 a.m. on the first day of the German invasion of France. Flight Lt Sammy Allard, the squadron's best pilot, is standing third from the right on the second row.

ABOVE RIGHT: Flying Officer Edgar J 'Cobber' Kain of No. 73 Squadron RAF, standing by his Hawker Hurricane Mark I at Rouvres, shortly after becoming the first Allied air 'ace' of the Second World War.

BELOW: Hurricanes of the fleet air arm, operating from Yeovilton, Somerset, December 1941.

ABOVE: Squadron Leader Douglas Bader (front centre) with pilots of No. 242 Squadron grouped around his Hurricane at Duxford, September 1940.

BELOW: Douglas Bader (centre) and fellow pilots study an emblem of Hitler painted on a Hawker Hurricane, October 1940.

being credited with shooting down thirteen aircraft. His overview of the battle is revealing and insightful.

'During the Battle of Britain we were flying about fifty, sixty, seventy flights a month, sometimes twice a day, sometimes three, four, five times a day. We spent a lot of time in the air. We didn't sleep at night. We slept by our aircraft in our clothes. You flew all day, every day, sometimes at night.

'Exhausting? Yes and no. Between the ages of nineteen and twenty-five the human frame can stand anything; at nineteen or twenty you get carried away by the enthusiasm of the moment, you're shooting at aircraft, they're shooting at you, if you're very lucky you get away with it.

'During those sixteen weeks of the battle my squadron lost eight chaps shot down and killed; another twenty were very badly wounded as a result of having to bail out. The Hurricane had the disposition that the fuel tanks were such that they caught fire readily in the air, a lot of people were terribly burned during fighting in Hurricanes – the Spitfire was not so bad.

'The Hurri was a cart-horse among race horses, really.

'The German Messerschmitt Bf 109 fighter was much better than ours [The Hurricane], a fully metal construction and a closed canopy, we only had .303 machine guns and in some respects their injections [of fuel] were much better than ours.

'A Bf 109 could knock a Hurri out of the sky with four shots, the Hurri might need forty. And, of course, they had been fighting in the air much longer than we had.

'There were 2,947 of us in the RAF during the battle, there were about 4,000 Germans, that's roughly a ratio of those that took part. We lost 1,100 fighters, Hurricanes and Spitfires, and we lost 550 men killed, 650 shot down and hideously wounded and burned. The Germans lost 1,700 fighters and bombers, but of course when they lost those, they lost the whole crew. A considerable loss for them over a period of sixteen weeks.

'Of course, Hitler had other fish to fry. He had at the back of his mind he was going to fight – in the not too distant future – Russia. He didn't want to waste all his aircrew fighting us.

'At the time of the battle, 249 Squadron comprised 200 people with twenty-two pilots and eighteen aircraft.

'No matter how many planes might be lost in one day, by the following lunchtime they would be up to full strength again. This level of organization and supply was a key to Britain's success in the Battle of Britain: the miracle of RAF organization, we could resupply ourselves.

'At nineteen, I was the first young officer to get to the squadron – the average of those who fought in the battle was twenty-one years and a couple of months.

'None of us had ever seen any action: we took it all in our stride, so most of the pilots were nineteen or twenty. This was what was expected of us, it's the job you do.

'I was paid 11 shillings and 9 pence a day [around 60p a day] – that was my salary as a junior officer; later, even as a test pilot, I was paid one pound nine shillings and sixpence a day.

'In a fighter squad you started work half an hour

before dawn – around 3.30 a.m. until half an hour after dusk, around 11.30 at night. Sometimes you flew the whole twenty-four hours.

'It was a draining business. Often during the end of a busy day, when you lost a lot of people, you were down to just five or six aircraft.

'We were never short of aircraft because of our organization to re-supply but we were short of pilots throughout the battle – and gradually the type of pilots changed, gradually all the squadrons throughout the air force were filled with voluntary reservists.

'There was a class division in the type of people in the squadron; you lived in separate messes, you drank in separate pubs, ate in separate areas.

'But gradually it changed. As regards the airmen looking after my aircraft on the ground, I was nineteen – and the two airmen looking after my aircraft were nineteen; those men kept in touch with me throughout our lives; you had a tremendous devotion to each other and they took as much pride in my achievements as I did myself – the pilot was "their" person so to speak and they looked after him and looked after his aircraft: it was very much a personal affair.'

August 1940 brought several memorable dates during the battle:

## 12 August

The Luftwaffe began their systematic assault on aerodromes in Manston, Lympne and Hawkinge in Kent, and radar installations in Kent, Sussex and the Isle of Wight. The airfields suffered different degrees of damage but were all serviceable by the next morning. Most of the radar stations were quickly back on the air with the exception of Ventnor on the Isle of Wight, which was seriously damaged.

These attacks displayed features that would characterize the fighting in the days ahead. They involved hundreds of aircraft timed to closely coincide with or follow one another, often on widely dispersed targets. Bombers, including the Junkers Ju 87 or the 'Stuka' dive-bomber, were heavily escorted by fighters.

Wherever possible, Spitfires took on the German fighters and the Hurricane would attack the bomber formations.

## 13 August

This was called 'Adlertag' (Eagle Day) by the Germans, and saw the first mass strikes on RAF airfields. It had been planned for 10 August but bad weather led to its postponement.

The Luftwaffe mustered a formidable force: medium bombers, dive-bombers, single-engine fighters and twin-engined fighters. Strong attacks over a ten-hour period were targeted against airfields, radar stations, Channel shipping, aircraft factories and manufacturing cities. Essex, Kent, Sussex and Hampshire came under attack.

The intention was to probe British defences; this turned out to be only moderately successful. Southampton experienced some damage, but the airfields at Odiham, Farnborough and Rochford were completely missed.

The day demonstrated, however, the difficulty British RAF defences had in meeting the Germans with forces large enough to inflict significant losses.

## 16–17 August

## AN AMERICAN IDEALIST

In the south-east corner of a church graveyard at Boxgrove, a village just a few miles from Chichester, there is a headstone dedicated to the memory of Pilot Officer William Meade Lindley Fiske III, better known as American pilot, Billy Fiske.

Fiske (1911–40) was the first US citizen to travel to the United Kingdom at the onset of the war to join the RAF. He was one of seven American pilots who flew in the Battle of Britain, at a time when America's wartime status was neutral.

The son of a successful international banker, Fiske attended boarding school in Oxfordshire, then Trinity College Cambridge reading history and economics. He developed a love for Britain – and its people.

An accomplished sportsman, he led the bobsleigh team to a Gold Medal for the USA in the Winter Olympics of 1928 at age sixteen. He had tried his hand at motor racing and entered the Le Mans 24-hour event as a co-driver in 1930. He also financed a couple of Hollywood movies (including the first Hopalong Cassidy film).

After Cambridge, Fiske took up a post with the international bankers Dillon, Read & Co., working mainly in Europe. He first learned to fly at an aerodrome near London and married Rose Bingham, the former Countess of Warwick, in 1938.

That same year, in the wake of the Munich crisis, he volunteered for RAF service, returning to the UK to be interviewed and accepted by the RAF. Commissioned as a Pilot Officer in April 1940, he was posted to 601 Squadron at Tangmere on 10 July.

He was an above-average pilot and a fast learner. When he made his first flight with the squadron, he had never flown a Hurricane. His flight commander, Flight Lieutenant Sir Archibald Hope, described him as the best fighter pilot he had known, a 'natural' who learned how to fly in battle extremely quickly.

On 20 July, he undertook his first operational missions in quick succession in Hurricane L1951. Over the next twenty-seven days he flew a total of forty-two sorties going into combat several times a day. As the battle heightened in August, Fiske downed his first German aircraft. On one day, 13 August, he claimed three Messerschmitt Bf 110s.

On 16 August, a formation of Junkers Ju 87 Stuka dive-bombers were seen approaching from the south, clearly intent upon attacking Tangmere aerodrome. The Stukas, escorted by Me 109s, massed over the Isle of Wight. Then they closed in on Tangmere, across the water. Most of the Hurricanes of 1, 43 and 601 Squadrons were already in the air, but too late to block the attack on Tangmere. Ordered to intercept the enemy at 12,000 feet (3,657 m), the defending Hurricanes and Spitfires managed to destroy seven dive-bombers and the rest of the Ju 87s were pursued out to sea. But two Hurricanes had been shot down during the interception. One was flown by Billy Fiske, who had taken off at 12.25 hours in Hurricane PP3358.

The Stukas inflicted considerable damage on the airfield, their bombing proving extremely accurate. The pre-war Tangmere hangars were flattened, along with the officers' mess, the station workshops, stores, sick quarters and shelters. Five Bristol Blenheims, part of the fledgling Fighter Interceptor Unit, were wrecked. Seven Hurricanes and a Miles Magister were destroyed on the ground. Some forty vehicles were also wrecked in the raid.

The Luftwaffe bombs killed ten RAF ground staff and three civilians. One of these was Henry Ayling, a civilian builder, killed when the slit trench he was sheltering in received a direct hit from a Stuka bomb.

Billy Fiske's Hurricane's fuel tank had been hit by one of the Junkers' tail gunners. Although it quickly became engulfed in flames, Fiske brought his plane in to land, so that it could be saved. He was pulled out of the blazing cockpit by nursing orderlies. The Hurricane was repaired and operational again within a few days.

Fiske had received serious burns and was taken to the Royal West Sussex Hospital in Chichester. He died from his injuries the following day. His funeral took place with full military honours at Boxgrove on 20 August. In due course, a plaque was placed in St Paul's Cathedral to commemorate 'An American Citizen Who Died That England Might Live', an idealist who had defied neutrality laws to fight in humanity's cause.

On the day of Billy Fiske's funeral, Winston Churchill made a famous speech in the House of Commons referring to the efforts of the RAF crews in the Battle of Britain. 'Never in the field of human conflict was so much owed by so many to so few.' Since then, those who fought in the battle have forever been described as 'The Few'.

## A FRAGILE DAY-TO-DAY EXISTENCE

In addition to being killed in aerial combat, a pilot's life was at risk from Luftwaffe attacks on his airfield. These could pierce armour plating at a very short range. Bullets might hit fuel tanks or an oxygen bottle – causing the plane to explode in a ball of fire. Controls, equally, could be shot to pieces, sending the Hurricane into an uncontrollable spin. Engine failure was another possibility. Or the pilot might find it difficult to open the canopy if he needed to bail out – a problem with earlier Hurricanes. Even if he did manage to escape, the parachute might not open. Or a pilot might come down in a freezing cold sea and perish from hypothermia before any rescue attempt could be made.

In August 1940, eighty-five Hurricane pilots were killed, nearly seventy badly wounded. Almost half of just one squadron's Hurri pilots lost their lives during July and August. As the Battle of Britain dragged on, week after week, the fear of death was ever present at all times.

Harold Bird-Wilson (1919–2000) of 17 Squadron reflected on this afterwards.

'You read stories of pilots saying they were not worried when they saw little dots in the sky which gradually increased in numbers and grew in size as they came from the French coast.

'I maintain that if anyone says he was not frightened or apprehensive on such occasions then he is a very bad liar. You cannot help but get worried when you look around you and see eleven other aircraft and you look ahead of you and see hundreds of aircraft coming towards you, whether they be fighters or bombers.

'I don't believe that any man is that tough. I openly admit that I was worried, frightened at times. As the battle went on and on we were praying for bad weather, we prayed mighty hard. But somehow during the whole of the battle we had beautiful weather – sunshine and blue skies.

'But fatigue broke into men's mentality in the most peculiar ways. Some got the jitters and facial twitches. Others, as I did, had nightmares at night. I used to wake up in the dispersal hut, sleeping within 25 yards [23 m] of my aircraft, after imagining that I had been night flying my Hurricane. This went on for quite a long time.'

Harold recalled a vivid memory of attacking formations of more than a hundred enemy aircraft as one of a force of only twelve Hurricanes:

'Your throat dried up as you got nearer.'

Bird-Wilson became one of the war's most celebrated airmen, an Air Vice Marshal, CBE, DSO, DFC and Bar, AFC and Bar.

The son of a Bengal tea planter, he was sent to boarding school in England at age four. He joined the RAF on a short service commission in 1937, being assigned to 17 Squadron at Kenley in August 1938.

While on a navigation course later that year, he was piloting a BA Swallow (a light civilian aeroplane) when the plane ran into a storm and crashed in bad weather. His passenger was killed but 'Birdie', as he was later nicknamed, survived the crash with severe facial injuries, so badly burned he was left without a nose.

He became a very early patient of Sir Archibald McIndoe, the New Zealand-born surgeon whose pioneer treatment of the Second World War burns victims, especially Hurricane pilots, went on to revolutionize the field of plastic surgery (see pages 107–8).

Following several operations by McIndoe at the Queen Victoria Hospital, East Grinstead, Birdie – undaunted –

converted to Hurricanes at the end of 1939, before re-joining 17 Squadron in February 1940. By April 1940, with his face fully restored, he was back on active service flying Hurricanes in France during May and June, covering the Allied retreat from France.

During the Battle of Britain, the twenty-year-old shot down six enemy aircraft in his Hurricane. But then, on the morning of 24 September while flying Hurricane P3878 near Chatham, he was shot down by Adolf Galland in his Me 109. Galland was a top-scoring German pilot (one of the few to survive the war).

Bird-Wilson's Hurricane fell blazing into the Thames estuary. He recalled later:

> 'I knew I'd been hit. Flames came into the cockpit, the hood Perspex was all gone. I pulled the hood back and leaped out. Two of my section orbited around me. I was burned but picked up by a naval motor torpedo boat.'

After more time in hospital, he returned to active service in November 1940. With some shrapnel still lodged in his head he went on to claim another five victories during the war.

Birdie remained with the RAF in a number of high-ranking posts until his retirement in 1974.

## THE HURRICANE BURN

The early Hurricane Mark I, many of which were operational during those summer months of 1940, carried with it a specific risk for pilots: that of being badly burned.

First designs of the Hurri did not carry armour around

its fuel tanks. Nor did the fuel tanks 'self-seal' if they were punctured, something that later became standard during the Second World War. The doped fuselage and wooden frame could also catch fire easily. Fuel would flow from damaged tanks in the wings to an empty space under the cockpit.

A bigger problem was the main fuel tank, because it sat directly in front of the cockpit. If it was ignited, it shot a jet of super-heated flame directly into the pilot's face.

Some of the more experienced pilots at the start of the Battle of Britain had originally flown biplane fighters in the 1930s – and they tended to fly with the canopy open. Early Hurricanes had a problem with carbon monoxide fumes leaking into the cockpit. With an open canopy, if a pilot took off the uncomfortable oxygen mask, the oxygen could add to any fire in the Hurricane cockpit, raising the temperature by several thousand degrees. It was like turning the cockpit into a blast furnace. In such a situation, Hurri pilots often had only a few seconds to get out of the cockpit or face life-changing injuries – or worse.

## THE TOWN THAT DIDN'T STARE

Many Battle of Britain pilots with severe burns around the eyes and on their hands were treated by Sir Archibald McIndoe (1900–60) and his team at their special surgical unit at East Grinstead in West Sussex.

McIndoe used pioneering plastic surgery on pilots with severe burns. His programme revolutionized burns care. He had discovered that saline water treatment helped burned skin heal more quickly, after noticing that shot-down pilots who had been rescued from the English Channel tended to recover faster than those who went down over land.

Some pilots might require years of medical treatment for their injuries, but McIndoe also realized that treating the mental effects of these injuries was as essential as treating the physical. Pilots were allowed to wear normal civilian clothes or their uniforms while they were recovering and encouraged to leave the hospital grounds whenever they wanted.

The locals were asked to invite the pilots into their homes and ignore their injuries. Consequently, East Grinstead became known as 'the town that didn't stare'.

Pilots who benefited from McIndoe's far-sighted approach set up their own drinking society called The Guinea Pig Club, which had seven hundred members at one stage. The club held annual reunions until 2007. Some members lived to witness their hundredth birthday.

## 'THE BEST OF THE YOUNG'

From a very early age, Frank Walker Smith (1917–41) was obsessed with flying, but his hopes of joining the RAF were dashed when he failed an initial eye medical.

He didn't give up. Frank was at the head of the queue in 1937 to join the RAF Volunteer Reserve at his home town in Derby. Frank had already completed an engineering apprenticeship at Rolls-Royce when he started flying training on weekends at Desford, near Leicester. When the Volunteer Reserve was mobilized in September 1939, he joined the Flying Training School; then, in March 1940, he went into the RAF Operational Training Unit.

He was posted to 85 Squadron in France for a short time,

but, lacking replacements for lost or battered Hurricanes, the squadron was ordered back to base in May 1940.

Frank's first operational flight was on 18 June, flying Hurricane N2557 on convoy patrol.

On 18 August, his squadron was at the forefront of the Battle of Britain. Of 85 Squadron's eighteen pilots, fourteen were shot down – some twice – in the following two weeks.

On 26 August, twelve Hurricanes were scrambled to patrol the Maidstone area. Frank's combat report read:

'At approx. 1500 hours the squadron was ordered to scramble. At 15.27 we sighted eighteen Dornier 215s flying in a stepped-up formation. The whole squadron delivered a frontal attack led by the CO. On the second attack (another frontal) the bottom section of three broke away from the main body. This section was attacked again by myself and F/O Woods-Scawen. The Dornier 215 at which both of us aimed, broke formation and both of us attacked it at the same time. Bits were seen to break off and the starboard motor emitted black smoke. The plane then went down in a long glide and disappeared into the clouds. My bursts were of two and three seconds' duration.

'Claim: Half Dornier 215 destroyed.'

The combat report after another action on 28 August on the last of the day's patrol reads:

'At 1600 hours the squadron was ordered to patrol forward base.

'On reaching the coast, twenty Me 109s were spotted in the east. The squadron attacked in formation, but split up as it did so. I picked out one Me 109 and gave it a two-second burst as it crossed my bows 200 yards [183 m] away. It then dived into a cloud and I followed. I then noticed it crossed a gap and climbed up again. Staying in the top layer of cloud, I opened up and drew up to within 200 yards of him, and slightly underneath him.

'As I manoeuvred into position I gave him a five-second burst and noted the shots to be penetrating. After about four seconds, the port petrol tank was seen to burst and the machine then wobbled slightly and went into a steep dive.

'At that exact moment I was shot at from behind and had to do a steep turn to the left to avoid being shot down. As I pulled out of this I was in the cloud and decided to go and see if I could find what happened to my previous opponent. He had dived steeply through the clouds and as I came through I saw a large explosion on the sea surface and a large black cloud of smoke arose. On arriving back at base P/O Hodgson and P/O Hemingway confirmed that they watched a 109 dive straight into the sea and it was the splash that I saw. I climbed up again but could not find any more enemy aircraft.

'Claim: one Me 109 destroyed.'

The following day, Frank took off with eleven other Hurricanes to patrol over Hawkinge. At 4 p.m. they spotted eighteen enemy bombers escorted by thirty Me 109s. Though at a lower height, they climbed hard to follow the enemy aircraft. Between Beachy Head and Hastings more enemy appeared.

The pilots' reports logged Me 109s, Me 110s and Dorniers: the total estimated hostile aircraft was three hundred. The tiny band of twelve Hurricanes flew into the sun to gain height and to try and attack from above and behind. But more 110s appeared from their rear.

Frank was hit from behind, probably by an Me 109. He was injured in the right foot and, as he took evasive action, his plane dived steeply, Frank finding no response to the throttle or rudder controls. He bailed out at 1,600 feet (488 m) and parachuted down safely at Hawkhurst. He was treated and lost the little toe of his right foot. He returned to the squadron that evening.

Remarkably, his Hurricane, which crashed at Underwood Farm, Etchingham, was partially recovered by the local aviation society and is exhibited at Robertsbridge Aviation Museum, East Sussex.

Frank was not in combat again during the Battle of Britain. After a well-deserved break, the squadron began night-flying missions. These proved difficult in the dark skies of winter.

In February 1941, the squadron were re-equipped with new twin-engined night fighters known as the American Havoc 1 Night Fighters, which had a crew of three. Frank first flew one of them on 25 February.

He was promoted to Pilot Officer on 6 March. On 13 March, he joined Flight Lieutenant Sammy Allard, the squadron's best pilot, and New Zealand Pilot Officer 'Ace' Hodgson on a delivery flight to Ford to collect a new Havoc for the squadron.

At dispersal there were some difficulties fastening the last of the six Dzus fasteners used to secure the gun panel on the nose of the Havoc. It was thought it had been fastened, but when the Havoc became airborne the gun panel became detached and flew back, lodging behind the edge of the tail fin. This forced the tail down and, as the aircraft climbed, it stalled, then smashed into a field at Mill Field Ley, bursting into flames. All three occupants were killed.

On 29 September 1941, Frank was posthumously mentioned in despatches for the 'gallant work he performed during the Battle of Britain'.

In 1985, in a letter to Frank's family, Wing Commander Peter Townsend wrote:

> 'I have a clear and sympathetic memory of him when I took command of 85 Squadron. He was nice looking with a smile on his lips and a subtle sense of humour. He was an excellent pilot too. Three of these great young men were killed. We in the squadron felt their loss deeply. It is so sad for me to have to recall these memories. But war takes away so many of the best of the young.'

## 'FREEDOM, HONOUR AND FAIR PLAY'

On 17 June 1940, twenty-three-year-old Bill Millington was posted to his first operational squadron, 79 Squadron at Biggin Hill. He'd recently completed training on the Hurricane at the operational training unit at Sutton Bridge.

William Henry Millington (1917–40) was an Australian born in England's Newcastle upon Tyne in 1917. His family moved to Adelaide, South Australia, when he was aged nine. He was an active, sport-mad youngster with a noticeable ability to fix mechanical devices. He was also fascinated by flying. With war looming in June 1939, he returned to England on an RAF short service commission.

After his first successful sortie on 9 July 1940, he went on to destroy nine German aircraft.

On 31 August – a few days after he had attacked a formation of about sixty Heinkels, two of which he destroyed – his Hurricane, P3050, was set alight in combat over Romney. He crash-landed on Conghurst Farm, Hawkhurst, wounded in the left thigh and badly burned. Rather than bail out, he steered his Hurricane away from a village. He managed to get out before the petrol tanks exploded.

On 19 September, Bill was posted to 249 Squadron at North Weald. He claimed a Ju 88 destroyed and another shared on 27 September, with further shared or damaged aircraft on 29 September.

On 30 October, he was in combat with enemy fighters in Hurricane I V7536. No. 249 Squadron was patrolling North Weald aerodrome at midday at 20,000 feet (6,096 m). A number of Messerschmitt 109s were sighted at 28,000 feet (8,534 m). The enemy aircraft scattered and individual chases ensued. It was thought that groups of 109s repeatedly flew out to sea, then turned back again, perhaps hoping to entice others out to sea.

Tragically, in the ensuing action over the Channel that day, Bill Millington disappeared. He was declared 'missing' for several months; later, it was presumed he had been killed.

Tom Neil (see pages 96-9) remembered that October day as 'a miserable, bitty and perfectly bloody day'. Tom had taken off on the same patrol, but had to return to base with engine trouble.

Bill's disappearance affected everyone in the squadron. He'd been well liked. Many in the squadron had adopted squadron mascots. Bill had been attached to his two: a little dog he'd named Pipsqueak and a duck named Wilfred.

Tom Neil recalled:

'In dispersal Pipsqueak and Wilfred wandered around, mournful reminders of their absent master. If only they knew! But perhaps they did.'

Afterwards, Bill Millington's parents, William and Elizabeth, received a letter, written by a Miss Celia McDonald from Scotland. She wrote:

> *Bill entrusted this letter to me a long time ago and I have not sent it to you sooner because I knew you had such a strong feeling that he would still turn up and, like you, I hoped and hoped. But now they tell me from the Air Ministry that since so many months have passed without news of him we must presume that he was killed. You, his mother, can indeed be proud of him and I, one of his many friends, can be grateful for his trust and affection for the inspiration and help I gained from his great unselfish spirit.*

Here is the letter written by Bill Millington, also known as 'Terrier'.

My Dear Parents,

I have asked Miss McDonald who has been a particularly good friend to me, to forward this short note, together with any of my personal effects you may desire in the event of some untoward incident.

The possibility of a hasty departure from this life is ever present. I have endeavoured to adjust my personal affairs as well as possible under the circumstances.

I go forth to battle light of heart and determined to do my bit for the noble cause for which my country is fighting.

Having studied the subject from all angles, I am certain that freedom, liberty and democracy will eventually prove victorious whatever the cost.

I am proud of my country and its people, proud to serve under the Union Jack, and regard it as an Englishman's privilege to fight for all those things that make life worth living, freedom, honour and fair play – the things which have made our Empire what it is today.

Since leaving home I have endeavoured to live up to those standards dictated by honour and chivalry, one I am sure that I have not failed you. For any sorrow or suffering I may have caused, I sincerely apologise, but please do not grieve over my passing. I would not have it otherwise.

Flying has meant more to me than just a career or means of livelihood.

The companionship of men and boys with similar interests, the intoxication of speed, the rush of air and the pulsating beat of the motor awakes some answering chord deep down which is indescribable.

Farewell,

Your loving son,

Bill

Thirty-two Australians fought in the battle. Nine of these pilots became Aces. Thirteen were killed.

## A WAAF AT HENDON

Joan Rice (1919–2009) was a WAAF, nineteen when the Second World War began. Her time at RAF Hendon led to her frequently socializing with the young Hurricane pilots of 504 Squadron – men who went into battle knowing that only that night mattered, because their tomorrows carried no certainty at all.

Back in 1940, RAF Hendon was not a permanent squadron fighter base, but an all-grass airfield from which 504 Squadron flew for three weeks from 5 September to 23 September. (There is a replica of a Hurri Mark I, adorned with the colours of 504 Squadron who flew Hawker Hurricanes during the hardest phase of the Battle of Britain, and is sited at the entrance to the RAF Museum, London.) Joan was twenty at the time, working as a WAAF trainee at Hendon, after signing up to join the WAAF as a typist just after war broke out. She kept a written memoir of her thoughts and experiences at RAF Hendon in the years from 1939 to 1942. Much of what she wrote described the men she met, the clubs she went to, the nights out with friends, young service women living through the utter chaos of wartime, as well as the many air raids she lived through during her time there.

On 7 September 1940, just two days after 504 Squadron had arrived at Hendon, she watched Hurricanes taking off at every angle, landing, flying in formation, returning to refuel, dipping and twisting and rolling over her head. In the background came the heavy boom of guns and a nearby burst of machine-gun fire.

After the All Clear sounded following an air raid, she would count the numbers that were arriving back. Were there fewer planes than went out? she would wonder. By the end of 504's three-week sortie at Hendon, seven of the officers she had known there had been killed in action.

The young woman wrote that she was grateful she didn't have a pilot as a husband or a lover, given what it must mean living with apprehension all the time. Yet what she understood through knowing these men – as they partied and drank together in the precious night-time hours on the ground – was why they seemed so hard and self-sufficient. She realized this was the only way they could cope with the constant danger and pressure.

'How can any of them be blamed for their ruthless living, their desperate cramming of every sensation into hours when instead of gentle years they have only the rushing days?' she wrote.

Later, she observed: ' I have had all I ever want of the heady glamour of the operational pilot with his restlessness and his charm, his lust for good times and drinks and parties, his heartbreaking elusiveness of spirit and his sudden death.'

Her wartime memoir ended in 1942 after meeting her husband-to-be, Hugh Gordon Rice, who had served with the Eighth Army. The couple were married for forty-six years. They had three sons, Tim, Jonathan and Andrew. Tim is the well-known lyricist and author, Sir Timothy Rice.

The air war over southern England raged for nearly four months. RAF Croydon's fighter squadrons were in the thick of the battle. On 15 August, the base suffered massive bombing attacks on its airfield, surrounding factories, armoury and local homes. Three days later, the Luftwaffe launched an all-day offensive aimed at eradicating the RAF, targeting RAF Kenley and Biggin Hill.

## 'THEY FELT SAFER HAVING US THERE'

Jeff Brereton (1921–) was nineteen when he arrived at RAF Croydon with 605 Squadron at the end of September 1940. He had qualified as a flight mechanic earlier that year.

Croydon had already suffered so badly from bombing. Jeff, pilots and ground crew were housed in bungalows – from which residents had been evacuated – in nearby Wallington. Aircraft were based in a field behind the bungalows.

The squadron had twelve Hurricanes and twelve pilots. The field had two tents, one for the pilots as they waited for the order to scramble, the other for ground crew. The squadron flew five sorties a day.

> 'It was successful before I arrived – at least one pilot had shot down five aircraft. That said, we were now losing pilots and aircraft; we often had to fly undermanned until replacements came in.'

The Hurris were often returning with their airframe, made of steel with wooden forms attached to it, covered in linen, pockmarked by bullet holes.

> 'We had the job of cutting a piece of canvas to cover the damage and we had two tins of quick-drying synthetic camouflage paint, which was used to attach the canvas to the aircraft.
>
> 'There was only one petrol tanker and oil bowser (for aircraft refuelling), so it was quite a rush to get the aircraft serviced in time for the next take-off.
>
> 'Often the aircraft took off while the paint was still drying and it was common to see an airman stretched out across the

tail plane helping to keep the rear wheel down on the ground.

'As all our Hurricanes were new, we didn't have to do routine servicing: major work was done at our parent aerodrome at Kenley.

'Of the twelve Hurricanes that started [with the squadron] at the beginning of September 1940, only one survived, R118 UP-W, though it was badly damaged. I worked on it until the end of October 1940, when it left for major servicing.

'On arrival I was told that there were no formalities, we all had a job to do and that was to work together. Both pilots and ground crew were constantly changing, so from one day to the next you had no idea who you would be working with, but this allowed us to share our learning and experiences.

'Our relationship with the Battle of Britain pilots was different to at other times because of the urgency and losses. We often didn't know who would be flying until he was running towards us.'

To help raise the morale of local families, Jeff and his crew colleagues were encouraged by the squadron to go into the town of Wallington and share air raid shelters with them at night.

On his first visit with a colleague, Jeff came across two schoolgirls just as aircraft were heard approaching.

'We all sheltered behind a brick wall and fortunately the bombs dropped a little distance away. My friend escorted one of the girls back to her home and I escorted the other. Her mother was so pleased to see her girl home safely, she invited me in for tea. I stayed with them that evening in their Anderson shelter, leaving in time to be back for dawn patrol.'

This became a regular occurrence until the end of October when the air raids lessened.

It was Jeff's first time away from home and he enjoyed socializing with the families and their neighbours, playing party games and making the most of each other's company. In his RAF uniform he was a most welcome visitor – and a somewhat reassuring sight.

When it was time for the squadron to leave in February 1941 to move to Martlesham Heath near Ipswich, the local residents were very upset.

'They felt safer having us there during the bombing. The squadron put on a going-away party in the airport's country club and invited the locals. So much emotion was expressed that day, one would have thought that the war had finished.'

Jeff continued to be moved from place to place with his squadron. In September 1941, he was promoted to Leading Aircraftman and posted to 32 Squadron, which was also equipped with Hurricanes.

His squadron was posted abroad at the end of 1942, and from then on the squadron moved from country to country: Gibraltar, Algeria, Italy, Greece and then the desert in Palestine when the war finally ended.

Jeff left the RAF in 1946 and joined the National Fire Service that same year. He spent his entire career firefighting in Staffordshire, retiring in 1981 as Assistant Chief Fire Officer. He continued to be closely involved with both the RAF Association and the Fire Fighters Charity throughout his long life.

When opportunity presented itself, as it did in 2020, at the anniversary of the Battle of Britain, Jeff was proudly reunited with the Hurricane Mark I – the very same aircraft he had serviced during the Battle.

(Jeff's wartime story is abridged from an original interview published in *Air Mail* magazine, the members' magazine of the Royal Air Forces Association, rafa.org.uk.)

# CHAPTER 4

# A CHANGE OF FOCUS

Even relatively early in the Second World War, the presence of the Hurricane lifted spirits; a morale raiser, if you like. The 'two heads are better than one' maxim applies well to the two fighter planes (Hurricane and Spitfire) that so frequently operated together. It was a uniquely successful partnership – with the Hurricane achieving maximum advantage in its Mark I incarnation.

How did pilots view both fighters?

## 'THEY WERE BOTH LOVABLE'

Geoffrey Page (1920–2000) was born into an aviation family. His uncle, Sir Frederick Handley Page, headed Handley Page, a leading aircraft manufacturer founded before the First World War. From an early age, he developed a fascination with aircraft, but he was discouraged from adopting a career as a pilot by his father and uncle. They encouraged him to consider engineering instead.

While studying engineering at Imperial College he joined the University Air Squadron and quickly proved to be a competent pilot. Two weeks after war broke out, he joined the RAF as a pilot officer.

In May 1940, he was posted to 66 Squadron. He believed he would be flying Spitfires, which he'd already flown. But there had been a 'mistake' and he should have been posted to 56 Squadron at North Weald, flying Hurricanes during the Battle of Britain. So he went to North Weald.

'I was lucky because I had the unique experience of being one of the very few pilots during the battle who had flown both the Hurricane and the Spitfire. They were both lovable but in their different ways – they were delightful aeroplanes.

'I tend to give an example of the bulldog and the greyhound, the Hurricane the bulldog, the greyhound the Spitfire. One's a sort of tough working animal and the other one's a sleek fast dog.

'If anything the Hurricane was slightly easier. It wasn't as fast and didn't have the rate of climb. But during the battle what evolved was that the Hurricanes would attack the German bomber formations and the Spitfires, because of their extra capability of climbing, they would go up and attack the German fighter escorts. But in the earlier stages I found that we were getting involved with both bombers and fighters when flying Hurricanes.'

The Battle of Britain itself entered its second phase in the weeks following 24 August to 6 September as the Luftwaffe persistently bombed south-east airfields in its attempt to clear the RAF from the skies over Kent and Sussex – and to prepare the way for what the Germans planned to be an invasion in the areas between Dover and the Isle of Wight.

During this time – up to 6 September – aircraft losses were at their peak and 562 German aircraft were destroyed. Britain's losses at that time totalled 219 fighter planes – from which 132 pilots were saved.

Fortunately, several more Hurricane squadrons became operational, including two Polish, one Czech and one Canadian, flying Canadian-built planes. Yet by then, more than two hundred and eighty pilots had been killed or seriously wounded and over four hundred and fifty aircraft had been lost or put out of action.

## REPAIRING DAMAGED HURRICANES

Repairing the damaged Hurricanes was crucial by this point. The repair scheme, devised to bring such planes back into service if they were declared 'unrepairable', was set up by the Hawker design office.

Repairs to battered Hurris by ground staff were made somewhat easier by the Hurricane's simple design, but of course, they were often extremely difficult to make if the airfield itself was already under attack.

In some cases, repairs were carried out by field working parties despatched from the Hawker factory, especially if the Hurricane had come down in open country. The company would initially ascertain the extent of the repairs needed from an external repair source, i.e. an aircraft factory or engineering works. Then it would supply any requisite equipment to one of the field working teams. These dedicated men would spend every day of the Battle of Britain touring the country, salvaging and repairing crashed Hurricanes. In July, August and September 1940, thirty 'unrepairable' aircraft were repaired on site. From June to October, 661 Hurricanes were put back into service by teams from maintenance units, specially formed repair units and Hawker working parties.

## PROTECTING THE FACTORIES

The Hawker Hurricane factory sites did not escape the Luftwaffe's attentions, though they mostly escaped serious damage.

When a bombing raid on 3 October hit the Kingston plant, bombs destroyed much of the Hawker design office, killing a workman on fire-watch duty.

The Hawker design experimental and admin teams had been moved to Claremont House, Esher, away from the areas bombed, a sensible precaution because a near miss had also destroyed the First Aid Centre at Hawker's Canbury Park Road premises. As for the Kingston production lines, Hurricane production was not affected.

On 4 September, a heavy raid was directed at the Hawker factory. As the Messerschmitt Bf 110s neared their target, they were met by Hurricanes of 253 Squadron, which shot down six of them.

The onslaught continued but, disoriented by the Hurricane intervention, the Bf 110s bombed the wrong aircraft factory. This caused damage to the Vickers factory (which was making Wellington bombers and had to cease production for four days), while the Brooklands Hawker factory remained untouched. The three-minute attack on the Vickers factory, however, resulted in 700 casualties, with nearly a hundred of them fatal.

On 6 September, the Hawker works at Brooklands were again

targeted. Once more, the Hurricanes of 1 Squadron intercepted the Messerschmitt Bf110s and shot down two. A bomb fell through the roof of the so-called 'New Shed', but caused little damage. Subsequently, the Hawker works managed to increase Hurricane production deliveries by 10 per cent that month.

The Hawker factory at Langley, Slough, was also attacked, yet damage to the new wing-assembly area turned out to be limited.

As an insurance against Hawker Aircraft losing everything in a bombing raid, vital components had previously been dispersed to various local premises, commandeered under wartime powers. Benaters – a large garage at Surbiton, not far from the Hawker Kingston factory – was one such storage facility. At one stage, several thousand Hawker Hurricane undercarriages were stored there.

But while Hawker sites escaped serious damage, Hawker Aircraft lost one of their most valued test pilots in early September, in a most tragic twist of fate, just a few hours before he was scheduled to re-join Hawker Aircraft.

## HE FLEW TOO HIGH FOR TEARS

Richard Carew Reynell (1912–40) was born in Adelaide, South Australia, where his family owned a large winery. He had a military background. His father, Lieutenant Colonel Carew Reynell, had been killed at Gallipoli in 1915 while serving with the 9th Australian Light Horse. The Reynell family arrived in England in 1921 when Richard, known as 'Dickie', was nine years old.

Dickie subsequently passed the Oxford University entrance examination to read agriculture at Balliol College. He discovered a love of flying after joining Oxford University Squadron. He joined the RAF on a short service commission in 1931 and the following year he joined 43 Squadron at RAF Tangmere.

In 1938, he joined Hawker Aircraft as an experimental test pilot and was closely involved with the development of the Hurricane in its earlier stages. By that time he had established a reputation as an outstanding test pilot.

In July 1939, as war loomed, he flew the Hurricane Mark I at the International Salon of Aeronautics at Evere, Brussels, where his masterly display was a superb demonstration of the Hurricane's capabilities. Here was an ideal test pilot, with excellent technical knowledge of the early Hurri.

On 26 August 1940, he returned to 43 Squadron at Tangmere in order to evaluate the Hurricane's performance in combat. He was also appointed Flight Leader.

By 2 September he had already shot down an Me 109 and was credited with many other 'probables'. Yet by 7 September he had been recalled by Hawker Aircraft as a test pilot.

With his strong sense of duty, Dickie Reynell opted to remain with 43 Squadron to continue that day's flying. And on that same day, the Luftwaffe had shifted its focus from RAF airfields and factories and started to raid London in force.

Two days before, Hitler had directed his air fleets to begin a general campaign against urban targets. The German air force commanders had assumed that, by now, the RAF was a spent force. Therefore they could bring the rest of the country under attack in stages.

Late that summer afternoon, nearly 400 Luftwaffe bombers, escorted by more than 600 fighters, thundered overhead en route for London. This, their commanders believed, would be the final blow to break British defences.

Reynell and his squadron of 12 Hurricanes went on the attack against 100 German aircraft. At 16.45 hours, as he was approaching south London, Dickie Reynell was shot down by an Me 109. A long tail of smoke billowed behind the stricken aircraft.

It is not clear whether he had been wounded, yet he somehow managed to get out of the cockpit and jump before his Hurri exploded into flames. However, his parachute failed to open – if he had been wounded, he might possibly have been unconscious by then – and he fell to his death near Blackheath. His Hurricane V 7257 crashed nearby.

Dickie Reynell had recently married and his widowed wife, Enid Marjorie, gave birth to a son the following year. He was buried at Brookwood Cemetery, Woking. He was twenty-eight.

The inscription on his grave reads: 'A paladin among the guardian Few. You flew too high for tears.'

That day of Reynell's demise, Saturday 7 September, was known as 'Black Saturday', a bitterly fought day with losses of thirty-one aircraft, including six Hurricanes from 249 Squadron.

The attacks continued until dawn the next day as the German bombers kept up their assault on the capital, causing terrible devastation and killing nearly five hundred people across the city.

Yet the blackest of black days also proved to be a key turning point, as the Germans had switched their attack away from the RAF fighter stations, mistakenly believing them to be completely knocked out.

The RAF squadrons were certainly groggy and battle weary. Yet the tide had suddenly turned. The Luftwaffe's unexpected change in tactics delivered an important breathing space for Britain, a tactical mistake by the enemy – and one that would very soon cost them the Battle of Britain.

'When the airfields were being bombed we were at rock bottom,' recalled Sergeant Richard Mitchell of 229 Squadron, who flew Hurricanes from RAF Northolt in the battle. 'But the change to bombing the cities gave us breathing space. Once we started to build up again, it was a matter of time until the German defeat.'

The Luftwaffe raids on London continued. But the airfields and Dowding's control network continued to avoid much damage. The weather helped across the south of England in the week after Black Saturday, with drizzle and thick low cloud – and only minor Luftwaffe raids.

The airmen were now able to snatch some much-needed rest – and the important training of new pilots could be maintained at a steady pace.

Hurricanes were arriving from the factories too. In spite of everything – the damage, the deaths, the lowering of morale – by the middle of September, the RAF would boast more fighters than it had in the previous two months. In some cases, squadrons had a full complement of planes and pilots.

In Germany, the belief that Britain was poised for defeat still prevailed.


## 'A MOMENTOUS DAY'

On the bright, sunlit morning of 15 September, 200 Luftwaffe bombers, heavily escorted by fighters, assembled over the Channel.

They were met on their way to London by more than 300 Hurricanes and Spitfires. A total of 158 bombers reached London, but visibility was poor and the German bombs were scattered wide. Another large German offensive took place in the afternoon, made up of 150 bombers and 400 fighters staggered in three waves. Again, the RAF was ready for them.

Tom Neil of 249 Squadron called 15 September 'a momentous day'. He shot down a Dornier in the early afternoon.

'The whole of the port side of the German aircraft was engulfed by my tracer. The effect was instantaneous, there was a splash of something like water being struck with the back of a spoon. Beside myself with excitement, I fired again, a longish burst.'

Moments later, the German crew had to bail out. Soon afterwards, Neil joined with a Spitfire in taking down another bomber over Gravesend in Kent.

'It was easy. Without interference, we took turns in carrying out astern attacks and were gratified to see a translucent stain of dark smoke emerge from one, then both of the engines.

'Back at dispersal I found a queue of pilots leading to the intelligence officer, everyone in a state of high excitement.

'It had been a fantastic fight, no one missing and a mounting tally of Huns – seven – eight – nine "destroyed" and a similar number probable or damaged. What a to-do! Crashed Huns burning on the ground everywhere.'

The next day, the British press were ecstatic. It had been announced that 185 of the enemy had been shot down. 'It is the RAF that strikes like lightning and it is the Luftwaffe that is stricken', crowed the *News Chronicle* on 16 September. 'Our planes race out above the Channel – whose waters are as much ours as they have ever been – and rip Goring's bombers out of the skies so that they fall like flies before the onslaught of an antiseptic syringe.'

The hyperbole was exaggerated. In reality, 34 German bombers had been destroyed that day, another 20 extensively damaged and 26 enemy fighters shot down. For the Luftwaffe it was one of the worst days of the battle. The RAF had lost less than half their total.

As a landmark victory, the date has endured through the decades as the memorable achievement of the Battle of Britain, the day when Britain fought back – and won. Yet the air battles in the week between 7 September and 15 September were, in reality, all decisive days in turning the tide.

Ironically, 15 September had been the date agreed earlier by Hitler during August as the start of the ill-fated Operation Sea Lion, the plan for the total invasion of Great Britain. Enthusiasm for invasion was already waning by then. Hitler believed there was a chance that the air assault on London might prove decisive by itself. The Sea Lion plan was postponed on 17 September. Three days later, Hitler postponed it indefinitely.

A month later, Hitler ordered his forces to maintain the appearance of an invasion threat in order to keep up 'political and military pressure on England'. The German air force was ordered to attack military and economic targets. But the idea of total invasion had been buried for good. And the Luftwaffe increasingly suffered unsustainable losses in daylight raids.

On 16 September, German air fleets were ordered to begin the next phase of the battle. Air power, they still believed, would deliver their solution. On 18 September, Germany launched over 740 aircraft against England, and a further 850 on 27 September.

Every one of the twenty-eight RAF squadrons launched against them made successful interceptions.

## THE BATTLE OF BRITAIN

The victory won in the Battle of Britain was the Hurricane's victory.

On that day, 15 September, the Hurricanes had shot down more enemy fighters than all other aircraft – Spitfires, Defiants, Blenheim fighters and the like – and anti-aircraft guns put together. They have been credited with destroying 54 per cent of the attacking German aircraft during the battle.

Altogether, 67 RAF squadrons were involved in the battle, 35 Hurricane, 19 Spitfire and the remainder being Defiants, Blenheims, Gladiators and Beaufighters.

More than 1,700 Hurricanes flew in the battle and 80 per cent of all claimed victories were by Hurricane pilots.

Victory has its price, however, and the campaign cost the RAF 471 pilots killed, 242 of them Hurricane pilots and 149 Spitfire.

Air Chief Marshal Sir Harry Broadhurst considered himself 'very lucky' to have commanded a Hurricane squadron during the Battle of Britain. 'The debt which the whole civilized world owes to Sir Sydney Camm and his Hurricane aircraft is beyond my capacity to express,' he said.

Afterwards, the Spitfire frequently held the mantle in the public mind as having 'won' the battle, especially after the 1942 release of the movie *The First of the Few*, which told the story of the late R. J. Mitchell, the Spitfire designer.

'Many more Hurricanes than Spitfires were fighting in 1940 and to Sydney Camm rather than the late R. J. Mitchell goes the honour of designing the fighter which saved Britain from defeat', insisted the *Chelmsford Chronicle* in November 1942.

If the truth lies not in the perception but in the solid achievement of the Hawker Hurricane, it would be the

Hurri's heroic airmen who, to this day, would share the bulk of the accolades.

## THEY CALLED IT THE ISLAND OF LAST HOPE

They started to arrive in Britain at the end of 1939. Seven months later, 8,400 Polish airmen were on British soil.

Exhausted, tired from their defeat from Germany, the Polish pilots saw Britain as their only hope for the future – they named it 'The Island of Last Hope'.

Their defeat at home had been swift and devastating. On 1 September 1939, the German Army, Navy and Luftwaffe invaded Poland. On 17 September, the Soviets launched their own invasion from the east of Poland. The Polish pilots fought with distinction in the air. But their country was crushed by two invaders – in just five weeks.

After their defeat, tens of thousands of Polish servicemen made their way to France hoping to continue their struggle. When the Polish Air Force was re-created in France, the Polish airmen relished the opportunity to fight Germany again. Yet their combat experience and fighting ability were not recognized. Polish pilots were rarely deployed in combat. Then France, too, fell to the Germans.

Many Polish airmen were already in Britain early in June 1940. They were assigned to various squadrons. (After France's capitulation, the Polish Armed Forces, alongside the other Allied troops, had withdrawn all their units to Britain.) By August 1940, 8,400 Polish airmen were stationed in the country. They were hungry to fight.

At first the British had been sceptical about the flying skills of these men.

'All I knew about the Polish Air Force was that it had only lasted about three days against the Luftwaffe and I had no reason to suppose that they would shine any more brightly operating from England,' recalled Canadian Flight Lieutenant John Kent, an experienced fighter and test pilot who had joined the RAF in the 1930s.

Kent was posted as flight commander to the newly formed fighter squadron 303 (Polish) Squadron at RAF Northolt, which had been the very first operational Hurricane fighter squadron. On 2 August, the 303 Squadron arrived at Northolt, ready for training.

## THE LANGUAGE BARRIER

Some of the new pilots had to adjust to new equipment, i.e. the Hurricanes. Language was another important training issue. Many of the Polish pilots spoke French, German and Russian – but were not English speakers.

Johnny Kent started to learn basic Polish. He would then take the Polish pilots to squadron dispersal, point to aircraft parts and teach them their English names. In turn, the Polish men gave him the Polish names for these, which Johnny Kent wrote down and learned phonetically. It was a gradual start but eventually it was successful and he could communicate with the Polish pilots in the air.

Converting the pilots to the Hurri presented different issues. The pilots knew they were good. Mostly older than their RAF counterparts, they were fully trained, with an average 500 hours flying. They were certainly bringing valuable knowledge to air fighting. But they were undergoing a steep learning curve.

Recalled Johnny Kent later:

'Some of the pilots had never flown aircraft with retractable undercarriages. Also throttles worked in reverse direction, few had handled constant-speed propellers, the airspeed was indicated in mph instead of km/h, and the altimeter registered feet instead of metres. All this led to some interesting situations and, furthermore, our tactics were different – they had never heard of radar and interceptions controlled from the ground.

'I was amazed and very favourably impressed at how rapidly the Poles mastered these complexities, both pilots and ground crew.'

The Polish pilots at Northolt were impatient to get into action. They were well trained and 100 per cent motivated. By then, the Battle of Britain was in full swing. Finally, on 31 August, 303 Squadron was declared operational. At last the Poles could join the battle – on equal terms.

In the following weeks, 145 experienced, skilled Polish airmen fought in the Battle of Britain, 303 Squadron achieving an astonishing score of 203 enemy planes destroyed, – the highest-scoring Hurricane Squadron during the Battle of Britain.

On 7 September, 303's Hurricane pilots shot down fourteen enemy planes in one sortie over London – the first day of the Blitz – without a single loss on their own side. Nine of the squadron's pilots qualified as 'Aces'.

Trained to get in close, Polish airmen made the most of their .303-in (7.5-mm) machine guns and all the Hurricanes of 303 Squadron had their guns harmonized to converge at 200 yards (183 m) rather than the standard RAF convergence of 400 yards (366 m).

Yet they were not reckless. This is borne out by the fact that during the battle, the two Polish Squadrons, Nos 302 and 303, each lost only eight pilots, a figure much lower than that of most RAF units.

Pilot Officer Mirosław Feríc, of 303 Squadron, later described his experience of shooting down a Messerschmitt Bf 109.

'I caught up with him easily, he grew in my sights … it was time for firing. I did it quite calmly and was not even excited, rather puzzled and surprised to see that it was so easy, quite different from Poland when you had to scrape and try until you were in a sweat and then, instead of you getting the bastard, he got you.'

Afterwards, Squadron Leader Ronald Kellett recalled in the *Squadron Chronicle*:

We fought together through the great offensive of 1940 and I then knew that the pilots of 303 Squadron were not only the best but would also see me through any troubles. In the month of September, 303 Squadron was on top. No squadron from the Empire could equal the courage and skill of our pilots, no bombing could daunt our airmen.

## 'WE FOUND GRANDAD'S HURRICANE – SEVENTY-FIVE YEARS LATER'

Twenty-year-old fighter pilot Kazimierz Wünsche had a background very similar to many of the other Polish fighter pilots in 303 Squadron.

He had joined the Polish Air Force and graduated as a

fighter pilot in 1939. He fought briefly against the Nazis and escaped to France, via Romania. After France fell, he arrived in England on 22 June, just two weeks before the Battle of Britain began. Following RAF training in Blackpool, he was posted to 303 Hurricane Squadron on 2 August. On 31 August he claimed the destruction of an Me 109 and on 5 September he downed another.

The heavy Luftwaffe raids on London continued on 9 September, but the briefest lull in proceedings in daylight hours in the days after 7 September had given all squadrons much-needed breathing space.

At 17.25 hours on the afternoon of 9 September, Flight Sergeant Wünsche and 303 Hurricane Squadron flew off from Northolt on patrol. They encountered a large formation of forty Ju 88s escorted by a large number of Me 109s and Me 110s.

Johnny Kent shot down a Ju 88, which was seen to fall into the sea. Sergeant Frantisek destroyed an Me 109 and a Heinkel He 111 before crash-landing near Woodingdean, Brighton. His Hurricane was hit in the radiator, fuselage and port wing.

During the patrol, Sergeant Wünsche was shot down by an Me 109 over Beachy Head. He bailed out, landing near Devil's Dyke. His Hurricane, P3700, had crashed and burned out in farmland. The young man, slightly wounded in the leg and with some burns to his face, was admitted to Hove hospital. It would be June 1941 before he was able to return to combat.

In a remarkable twist of fate, part of Kazimierz Wünsche's crashed Hurricane – the Mark I P3700 in which he had flown so courageously during the Battle of Britain – would be revealed to his family seventy-five years later, in a moving reunion in 2015.

The farmland where the crash took place is owned by the National Trust, an important heritage site. The crash site had been located over forty years previously by amateur archaeologists. Most of the wreckage still lay in the ground.

With the collaboration of a team of aviation experts, the Army and archaeologists from the Ministry of Defence, a plan was evolved to fully excavate the crash site – and recover as much of the crashed plane as possible.

British and Polish veterans joined forces in the hunt for the plane, which was overflown on the anniversary of the crash by an original Hurricane, painted in Polish colours, organized by the Polish Embassy.

On the day of the excavation, a smiling Joanna Gasiorowska, Sergeant Wünsche's granddaughter, and Joanna's mother Grazyna Gasiorowska, stood proudly alongside the remains of the Hurricane's propellor hub.

'It was incredibly moving to see and touch part of his plane that hadn't been seen in seventy-five years,' said Joanna. Her mother had been taken back to Poland as a baby after the Second World War.

They had often wondered what had happened to the plane. 'He's remembered as a hero both here and in Poland, but I never got to know this incredible man who I am so proud of for his adversity and achievements,' added Joanna.

At RAF Northolt's Polish Museum, where 303 Squadron were stationed during the Battle of Britain, the remains of Joanna's grandfather's Hurricane are on display, a fitting testament to both 303 Squadron and one of the Hurricane's many Polish pilots who fought so bravely for 'the island of last hope'.

In the weeks that followed 15 September, the daylight raids on Britain continued. During that time, Britain's aircraft factories had taken the brunt of the air strikes. Production of the Spitfire was hit hard when the Supermarine plant in Southampton was bombed in late September. Brooklands took another hit on 21 September when a Junkers Ju 88 bombed the Hawker works. Three bombs exploded without damage; one with delayed action landed in the main Hurricane assembly shop and was removed safely.

While the Hurricane's vital contribution in the Battle of Britain was widely recognized in the aviation world, by autumn its success in the air battle was virtually overlooked by the general public, who had fallen heavily for the sheer glamour of the Spitfire, its look, its futuristic appearance. The 'Spitfire summer' theme had huge appeal. Spitfire funds were organized to raise money for the fighter and proved hugely successful. No such fundraising was even suggested for the Hurri.

On 26 September 1940, *Flight* magazine reported:

> People are taken in by the name and the appearance and the performance of the Spitfire. Knowing nothing of the performance figures they have instinctively chosen this particular type as the paragon of protective types, though any pilot will tell them that the Hurricane is equally remarkable in its own particular way … a machine, in fact, which has had far less than its due attention from a somewhat fickle public.

'Nobody loves us,' remarked one Battle of Britain pilot.

Aviation technology, however, was swiftly changing. Moreover, as the daylight battle began to end, the Hurricane, as a fighter, would be required to develop a different role.

This became evident early in winter 1940/41 when the Luftwaffe hardly ventured across the Channel in daylight, but would strike the country continuously at night. The main target was London, though Birmingham, Bristol, Coventry, Glasgow, Hull, Liverpool, Manchester, Portsmouth, Plymouth and Sheffield all suffered badly from enemy bombing.

In the last four months of 1940, 18,000 tons of bombs fell on London alone. In the seven months from September 1940 and May 1941, 40,000 civilians were killed – almost half of them from London.

## THE NIGHT FIGHTER

How could the RAF fight back during night-time? The only weapon likely to destroy the enemy was a night-fighter.

At the time, the RAF had very few night fighter units apart from the two-seater Boulton Paul Defiant Mark I. The Defiant had not proved effective against single-seat fighters, and since it carried both pilot and gunner, its casualty figures were worse than for other front-line fighter squadrons.

By late August 1940, two squadrons, 264 and 141, shared just seventeen Defiants. The plane was withdrawn from front-line service on 28 August and consigned to night fighting, where it did find some success until mid-1942, when it was replaced by better-performing night fighters.

The Hurricane, however, had not been designed as a night fighter. Yet it was initially thought that it could prove successful in the dark.

Five Hurricane squadrons, first 73 Squadron, then 85, 87, 151 and 96, converted completely to night-time operation. In practice, this idea proved ineffective. Without any navigational aids, Hurri pilots were literally flying in the dark.

Recalled Graham Leggett, now with 96 Squadron, a newly formed night-fighter unit based at Cranage in Cheshire:

'We had VHF radio, that's all. With the radio we could communicate with the ground controllers whose job it was to put us in a position to make an attack on an enemy bomber.

'But it all hinged on one's ability to see an aircraft in a dark sky. On a pitch-black night when there was no moon, it was virtually impossible to expect any form of contact at all.

'One night there was a huge fire in Liverpool and the glow lit up everything around; you would have thought it would have been easy to spot aircraft, but I didn't.'

Dennis David, 87 Squadron, felt that 'the idea of the Hurricane fighting at night in 1940 was an absolute waste of time because the approaching speeds were phenomenal. To see anything at night, with approaching speeds of six miles [9.6 km] a minute, just doesn't work. You've got to have AI.' (AI is Airborne Interceptor radar, which had only recently been developed.)

The German raiders releasing their bombs on Britain were virtually unchallenged by the Hurri. On the night of 14 November, when the Luftwaffe turned the centre of Coventry into a blazing inferno, the Hurricanes could do nothing to defend the city. Squadron Leader Douglas Bader led three Hurricanes of 242 Squadron over the city but saw only 'the sea of flame below'.

No. 85 Squadron flew more hours on night fighting than any other squadron in the three months to January 1941: they lost several aircraft in accidents due to bad weather. The squadron's Hurricanes, recalled Wing Commander Peter Townsend (1914–95), lacked the means for all-weather night fighting: radar, cockpit heating, de-icing equipment. Experience counted more than anything else. Weather, during winter, proved the greater hazard and killed more pilots.

However, by the spring of 1941, a series of innovations and events improved the night-time situation. By then, pilots had gained more experience in handling and tactics. A new lighting system – the Drem system (adopted throughout the RAF) – meant better landings by night. The arrival of the Bristol Beaufighter, a high-performance night fighter equipped with Airborne Interception radar, also flew successfully against the German raids.

Yet one Hurricane aviator stands out as one of the most skilled and successful of the Hurricane night fighters.

## THE LONE WOLF WITH CAT'S EYES

Flight Lieutenant Richard Playne Stevens, DSO, DFC and Bar (1909–41), had an exceptional attribute: he had superb night vision. A man who could identify planes when no one else could see a thing, he could land in airfields covered in fog, which normally grounded most pilots. He also possessed superb marksmanship.

Stevens's background was unusual, in that, aged thirty-two when the Second World War started, he was already much older than many airmen. Before wartime he'd flown extensively as a commercial pilot.

As a young man he worked on a cattle farm in Australia and a policeman in Palestine before his return to Britain in the mid-1930s. He then trained as a commercial ferry pilot with Northeast Airlines. Joining the RAF in 1937, he eventually trained on the Hurricane as a fighter pilot before being posted to 151 Squadron's night-fighter team at Wittering,

Cambridgeshire.

On the night of 15 January 1941, he claimed his first two kills. He spotted a Dornier 215 flying south over the London area and pursued it, unleashing fire. The Dornier returned fire, diving steeply. After a fifteen-minute chase, Stevens shot it down. It plunged to earth in a ball of flame.

Flying back to London, Stevens spotted a Heinkel at 17,000 feet (5,182 m) and took it out with a devastating burst from 50 yards (46 m), leaving it to crash into the sea off Canvey Island.

Stevens was awarded a DFC in February 1941. His citation reads: 'He shot down two hostile aircraft in the London area. In both these engagements he chased the enemy over 100 miles [161 km] before destroying them at extremely short range. In one instance he followed the enemy aircraft almost to ground level from 30,000 ft [9,144 m].'

In one daring operation in October 1941, flying at sea level, he intercepted and took out a Junkers 88 off the East Anglian coast.

His DFC citation for that engagement, dated 12 December 1941, reads:

> The raider immediately turned and flew towards the continent at maximum speed but Flt Lieutenant Stevens gave chase and slowly overhauled it. The raider then opened fire with his guns and began to drop his bombs singly. Columns of water shot up as a result of the explosions but Flt Lieutenant Stevens swerved round them and closing into short range shot down the enemy aircraft at almost sea level.

Afterwards he is reported to have said: 'I gave tally-ho, I've hit him. Tally-ho, he's going down. Tally-ho, he hit the ground with an awful thump.'

By June 1941 he had already shot down ten German planes. His reputation as a night flyer became the stuff of legend.

Stevens's colleagues found him a solitary and melancholy sort of man. If he was unable to fly, he would stalk around the officers' mess, avoiding talking to anyone.

On one occasion, after he had blown up a German bomber at point-blank range, the bloody remains of the German airman exploded across his Hurricane. His mechanic recalled:

> 'How he landed in the dark I don't know. The windscreen had a large hole in it. The oil tank was punctured and dented. We found hair and bits of bone stuck to the leading edge of the port wing. The tips of the propeller blades were covered in blood.'

## THE INTRUDER

By 1941, the night-fighter force started to inflict many losses. Following the devastating fire attack on London on 10 May, the Luftwaffe's mass night raids had all but stopped.

Stevens was then sent on intruder missions over occupied German territory to seek out the enemy. (Intruder missions were night-fighter missions aimed directly at German night-flying bases in order to destroy the enemy and their aircraft at their airfields. They were perilous, lonely assignments, but could have devastating results.) Stevens was a pioneer of intruder missions, the idea being in its infancy at that time. The quiet loner's success earned him another reputation: that he bore an intense hatred of the enemy. Some thought, mistakenly, that this was because he had lost his wife and children during the London Blitz.

Another 151 Squadron pilot, John Wray, recalled:

'He was a loner. He associated with virtually nobody. I was one of the few people who knew him at all. Steve's tactics were in accord with his character. He would take off from Wittering and, having got airborne, he would turn off his r/t [radio] and disappear into the night.

'Nobody knew where he had gone. He would then go into an area where he felt that there might be Germans approaching. Steve always said that while the British anti-aircraft guns could never hit anything, they were very good at tracking the enemy. So if he saw some British anti-aircraft guns firing, then in front was a Hun. Many of the Germans he attacked he picked up this way.'

Wray later admitted that he always felt that 'one day he [Stevens] would stick his neck out too far'.

Wray's instinct proved correct. In November 1941, Stevens had been posted to 253 (Hyderabad) Squadron as Flight Commander. The squadron was one of the first to introduce night-intruder flight, hunting at night over the enemy's aerodromes.

On the night of 15 December, climbing into his all-black Hurricane Mark IIC, Stevens set off from RAF Hibaldstow, Lincolnshire, on an intruder mission over Gilze-Rijen airfield in the Netherlands.

He failed to return.

The following day, the Germans discovered the wrecked Hurricane near the German airfield at Hulten. A Ju 88 wreck lay

600 metres (656 yards) from the Hurricane. Stevens had managed to shoot down the Junkers Ju 88 and damage another before he had flown too low and hit the ground. He was killed instantly. He was buried in Bergen-op-Zoom, just north of Antwerp.

He left behind a widowed wife, Olive Mabel, from whom he was estranged, and a son, John. The determined lone flyer with the cat's eyes had not, as some believed, lost his family in the Blitz.

## THE ARRIVAL OF THE MARK II

After the Battle of Britain the RAF had been immersed in balancing the huge issues around night flying and the Luftwaffe's devastating attack on Britain's cities.

But what of the Hurricane itself? Hawker Aircraft and designer Sydney Camm had understood from the beginning that the plane would soon need changes. At one stage in 1940 it was briefly mentioned – by government – that the Hurricane might be phased out.

This was never an option. The best course would be to enhance the Hurri's capability with greater engine performance and greater power for its guns.

In March 1940, Sydney Camm proposed the installation of a new engine on the Hurricane to the Air Ministry. Rolls-Royce had developed a more powerful version of the Merlin engine, the Merlin XX.

This delivered 1,300 hp (compared to 1,030 hp of the original). This meant stronger performance at altitude and improved the engine's efficiency: no design changes were needed other than a slightly longer front fuselage and a larger coolant radiator. Approval was given and Hawker started to produce a prototype of the Hurricane Mark II Series A.

In May 1940 it was agreed by MAP (Ministry of Aircraft Production) that the Hurricane IIA should have first claim over the Spitfire and the Beaufighter on the Rolls-Royce production of the Merlin XX engine – it was vitally needed to improve the plane's performance. It was also agreed that twelve Browning guns should be fitted to the newer version. Yet a shortage of Brownings during the battle resulted in some early Mark Is retaining the eight-gun version.

The first Mark IIA version flew at Hawker's Langley plant in June 1940, flown by Philip Lucas, Hawker's Chief Experimental test pilot. This achieved 348 mph (560 km/h).

The aircraft were immediately ordered into production. The cost would be £4,000 (equivalent to £238,000 – $286,619 – today). It was obvious the Hurricane needed the Merlin XX engine to keep pace in combat.

The new Hurricane would also be developed as a long-range fighter. Auxiliary fixed fuel tanks under the wings would be changed as 45-gallon tanks became standard on the new plane.

The various alterations could not, however, happen simultaneously. But it was clear that the new Mark IIA should be produced as soon as possible.

By September 1940, the first 120 models of the Mark IIAs Series I went into service with 111 Squadron, which had been the first to receive the Mark I. After heavy losses in the Battle of Britain, the squadron had withdrawn from combat. The new Mark IIAs were distributed as replacements to other squadrons as required.

A month later, the new Hurricane IIAs Series 2 arrived – this fitted with the new fuel tanks. These also had an extra fuselage bay and frame immediately forward of the cockpit, lengthening the nose by 7 inches (18 cm).

Through the winter of 1940–41, the IIAs went off to eleven Hurricane squadrons.

## THE MARK IIB AND FURTHER DEVELOPMENTS

From November 1940, Hawker had started production of the twelve-gun Hurricane, the Mark IIB. Three thousand planes of this version were built (more than the 3,857 versions of the Mark I, with just 415 of the Mark IIA).

The twelve-machine-gun arrangement of the Mark IIB increased fire-power (by 50 per cent) but in aerial combat the extra weight of the guns affected the rate of climb, lateral manoeuvrability and rate of roll. By mid-summer of 1941, IIBs were with twenty Hurricane squadrons.

The solution to the extra weight was to exchange the Browning guns for cannons, arming the Mark IIC with the Hispano 20-mm (0.8-in) gun.

Progress on this was slow, but by February 1941 production started on the Mark IIC. Weighing 8,100 pounds (3,674 kg), the standard Mark IIC was heavier than other versions, retaining a maximum speed of 336 mph (541 km/h). Its wing could carry bombs or long-range petrol tanks as well as the cannons. It went into service in the late spring of 1941, and by mid-summer, seven squadrons were equipped with the IICs.

The Mark IIC turned out to have the highest production run of any Hurricane. By 1944 it reached 4,711 constructed in Britain and Canada, the majority at Langley. It could be used in all manner of roles. But it was especially deadly against ground targets.

The last major variant to the Hurricane was the Mark IV (essentially a Mark II with a specialized 'universal' low attack wing). Hawker produced 524 of these. Armoured both internally and externally, they were the first Hurricanes to use air-to-ground rocket-attack projectiles in operations in September 1943.

Its use began in June 1943 with RAF 164 Squadron, against enemy shipping and coastal targets. The Mark IV was also used by six UK RAF squadrons and two in Burma (for combat use).

## 'KUT' THE NIGHT REAPER

The Hurricane IIC was flown by another remarkable high-scoring airman, Czechoslovakian Karel Kuttelwascher – a flyer who had arrived in England in 1940. He was a Battle of Britain Hurricane pilot who had already shot down three enemy planes in 1941. But what made Kuttelwascher a superb flying Ace was his outstanding skill as a night intruder.

Nicknamed 'Kut', he destroyed fifteen enemy aircraft, the greatest number of successful strikes of any RAF night intruder. At the time, his remarkable success became legendary: the wartime press dubbed him 'the Czech night hawk'. Kut's Hurricane IIC, his personal aircraft, bore a vivid emblem: a yellow scythe with a red banner emblazoned with the words 'Night Reaper' – altogether, a gruesome image reflecting his acute thirst for vengeance.

Kut had been enrolled as an RAF sergeant pilot in mid-1940. On 4 October 1940, he was posted to RAF Tangmere to fly Hurricanes. On 8 April 1941, operating from Kenley, he destroyed a Bf 109. On 21 May, he shared in the destruction of a second Bf 109, shooting down a third on 27 June.

In July 1941 he returned to Tangmere, converting to night-intruder operations, flying his cannon-armed Hurricane IIC with No. 1 Squadron.

On 1 April 1942, together with his squadron commander James McLachlan, DFC (2 Bars), he commenced night-intruder operations over enemy airfields in northern France. By 2 July 1942, 140 night-intruder operations had been flown by nineteen pilots.

During a three-month period, the Night Reaper flew fifteen trips, shooting down fifteen enemy aircraft, three of them in just one night. This won Kut two DFCs in just forty-two days.

In July 1942, his squadron was moved to Acklington. Afterwards, he went on to fly Mosquito night fighters. The following year he remained in England with an RAF staff appointment and undertook a lecture tour of the USA.

He returned to Czechoslovakia when the war ended, but with the advent of the Communist regime there, he returned to England in 1947. He became a pilot with British European Airways – but died of a heart attack in 1959 aged forty-two.

## THE HURRICANE WOMEN

A lesser-known fact concerning the Hurricane is that a third of Hawker Aircraft's manual workforce engaged in helping build it were women.

Women workers featured heavily in the production of Second World War aircraft, undertaking many of the jobs previously carried out by men, working long hours.

A production-line day shift for Hurricane workers at Kingston, for instance, would be from 7 a.m. to 6.30 p.m. (with a one-hour lunch break); the night shift entailed eleven and a half hours. All this at a time when air raid warnings in key areas such as the London suburbs were frequent.

In the Hurricane factories, women could be working on installing the bulkhead between the cockpit and the Merlin engine, or engaged in the meticulous task of securing the numerous electrical cables, hydraulic and fuel lines. They might be preparing the rear fuselage ribs for the fabric skin – or fitting the metal skins onto the wing ribs.

The long shift hours were typical of all those engaged across the country in the Second World War's armament production, including the largely unheralded wartime munitions workers, millions of whom were women. (For the munitions workers, it was often highly dangerous work, filling armaments with highly toxic materials.)

At the Hawker production line, the work itself was less hazardous – aside from air raid warnings – and the Hawker factories were very well run.

## AN UNLADYLIKE WOMAN

One of the very few women in a senior aviation engineering role in Britain during the Second World War was Beryl Platt, a senior technician at Hawker.

Baroness Beryl Platt (1923–2015) started life determined to succeed in areas deemed 'unladylike'. She completed an aeronautical engineering degree at Cambridge University. After a three-week placement at Hawker (where she shone among her somewhat stunned male counterparts), she joined Hawker's Experimental Flight Test Division in 1943, one of the first-ever wartime female aeronautic engineers.

Working alongside a team of fifty men, she refused to learn to type – thus avoiding any risk of secretarial work. Sixty-five- to seventy-hour working weeks were typical, working on the testing and production of some of Hawker's outstanding fighter planes, including the Hurricane, Tempest V, Typhoon and Sea Fury.

She recalled in 1989:

> 'It was very hard work. The atmosphere was intense and it was a very crowded production line. I always remember Hawker tea, which didn't taste of tea at all but it was hot and wet. Someone once told me they put bicarbonate of soda in it. But there was a great camaraderie. People did pull together and that's why I speak with such affection of the people I worked with on the shop floor. We knew we could rely on each other.'

After the war she moved to an engineering role in British European Airways, and in 1949 she married and settled into family life with two children. In her thirties she took on several prominent roles in local government, later being made a Conservative life peer by Margaret Thatcher. During her time in the House of Lords, she continued to pursue her lifetime goal: changing people's attitudes to women.

In an interview many years after the Second World War, she paid tribute to the Hurricane.

> 'Without those Hurricanes you and I would not be sitting where we are today.'

## THE WOMEN IN THE COCKPIT

But how were the brand-new Hurricanes delivered by air from the factory production line to the RAF fighter stations?

The answer was the Air Transport Auxiliary, a civilian organization, set up in 1939 to provide logistical support to the RAF.

As the production lines of brand-new aircraft increased rapidly during the war, ferrying new or repaired aircraft from factory to squadron stations or, in some cases, to repair sites, became an important part of the war effort.

It was launched in 1939 – initially as a male support to the RAF – promising to take 'any aircraft anywhere'. The ATA's female component began slowly, given the early resistance at the time to women pilots. Yet, thanks to the redoubtable efforts of Pauline Gower, Commander of the women's section of the ATA, female recruitment grew during wartime. Eventually, the ATA had 166 female ATA pilots, among them the well-known aviator Amy Johnson, killed on an ATA trip in 1941.

At first, there were few Hurricanes available to ferry, even though the Hawker factory at Langley was near ATA's first ferry pool at White Waltham, Berkshire. But on 19 July 1941, a Mark I Hurricane arrived there to enable the handful of women to carry out practice landings.

Winifred Crossley, one of the 'first eight' female ATA pilots, was the first female ATA pilot to fly the Mark I around one circuit.

Lettice Curtis (1915–2014) had joined the ATA in July 1940. At the end of July 1941 she was tasked with delivering a Hurricane Mark I from Dumfries to Prestwick, a short flight but nonetheless her first time in a fighter. (This was Hurricane L 1927 – a pre-war Mark I with a Merlin II engine.)

She recalled climbing in 'with a host of butterflies in my stomach'. She looked for the Pilot's Operating Handbook and checked the cockpit for relevant knobs, switches and levers. Compared to anything she had flown thus far, the cockpit seemed very tight and narrow – even her small overnight bag had to be stored under a panel in the wing – but she started up, taxied out and was in the air without incident.

Later, as a far more experienced ferry pilot (she handled nearly one and a half thousand aircraft of all types during her time with the ATA), she described the Hurricane as 'dogged, masculine ... its undercarriage folded inwards in a tidy business-like manner'.

Another early ATA flyer was Margaret Gore (1913–93). Already an experienced aviator, she joined the ATA in June 1940. She too flew a Hurricane for the first time in 1941. She recalled:

> 'I hadn't flown anything comparable to it. We really felt we were getting somewhere when it arrived, a real fighter, particularly because we had seen the Battle of Britain going on overhead the autumn before. It really was extremely exciting.'

But if the recent developments in the Hurricane's weaponry had achieved certain results, the plane was also considered for a number of other developments, several of which were mooted – but not adopted.

There were intangible but noteworthy gains, however. Hurricane raids over Nazi-occupied countries were one example. Some Hurricanes dropped propaganda leaflets through a chute on the side of the fuselage, formerly designed for the use of parachute flares at night.

The Hurricane's very presence in flight also demonstrated

that the RAF was powerful in the air. In Holland, people in village streets would doff their hats to the fighter plane. In Belgium, civilians would wave at them. As in the suburbs of London during the Battle of Britain, locals saw an RAF uniform as a reassuring and welcome sight. The Hurri was a beacon of hope.

There were inexpensive innovations too.

Batches of Hurricanes were built for just £50 ($60). These were dummy aircraft, made of wood and cardboard, placed on decoy airfields to completely mislead the enemy bombers.

They looked like the real deal – identical in shape and size to the real aircraft, over five hundred were constructed. To emphasize the deception, the mock airfields carried landing lights and flare paths. Nine of these fake stations existed in 1940 and 1941, all part of the RAF's decoy system of bases. A handful actually drew in German raids, some of the decoy aircraft were also despatched overseas to be used in the Mediterranean and North African bases.

## THE SUICIDE MISSIONS AT SEA

Perhaps the most extraordinary development of 1941 involving the Hurricane – which ultimately proved successful – was the 'Hurricat': a seaborne fighter Hurricane rocket catapulted from a ship to provide convoy protection against air attack.

German U-boat attacks on convoys in the Atlantic – travelling with desperately needed supplies – had become an extremely serious concern. The convoys were essentially alone, without air cover. A means had to be found to combat the long-range German Focke-Wolf 200 Condor aircraft. The Condor was extremely effective not only in locating convoys and calling in U-boats, but also in heavy bombing. It sank nearly a million tons of Allied shipping in just a few months. Could there be an airborne solution?

Enter the Catapult Armed Merchant ships, introduced in the spring of 1941. They were fitted with a launch rail from which Hurricats – catapult-launched Hurricanes – were given a rocket-assisted take-off while in mid-ocean. This was extremely hazardous. Many described these Hurricane missions as kamikaze or suicide missions.

These were single-use planes. They were not fitted for landings – there was nothing to land on. The pilot would have to ditch into the freezing cold sea at the end of the flight and hope to be picked up by one of the convoy. The plane would either be lost or perhaps recovered and hoisted aboard.

Initially, Hurricanes were converted by installing catapult spools and attachments, plus a heavily padded headrest as a shock absorber for the pilot. The rocket sled, designed for solid fuel rockets, was developed at Farnborough. Many of the pilots and maintenance staff recruited for the new Merchant Ship fighter unit – part of the Admiralty's Fleet Air Arm – came from the RAF.

## A HURRICAT TRAINING FLIGHT

The *London Evening Standard* newspaper of 26 November 1942 described the training flight. After the pilot gave the signal,

> 'the explosive charge is ignited and with a roar the cradle carrying the Hurricane hurtles along the "scenic railway track".
>
> 'Belching flame from behind, it gathers speed at 70 mph (113 km/h) or more as it dashes into the buffers at

the end of the railed track and shoots the catapulted fighter into the air.

'The Hurricane takes to the air with only a few feet to play with and usually dips a little as it leaves the catapult. Then it quickly gains height, does a few circles around the airfield and comes down, the practice flight over.'

That described an early training practice. But would a rocket-propelled fighter – the first of its kind – work in reality?

## THE FIRST 'KILL' BY A ROCKET-LAUNCHED HURRICANE

On 3 August 1941, Lieutenant Robert Everett volunteered to test the first rocket-launched fighter. He was a colourful figure. Born in Australia in 1901, he had been an amateur pilot and a superb jockey, winning the Grand National in 1929. He also jointly owned, with his father, a de Havilland Puss Moth. He joined the Royal Naval Volunteer Reserve and Fleet Air Arm in October 1940 and later volunteered for 804 Naval Air Squadron, supplying pilots for fighter catapult and CAM ships.

On that memorable August day, a Condor was sighted and he was launched from CAM ship *Maplin*. The patrolling Condor didn't seem to see the launch but reacted, severely damaging the Hurricat. Despite heavy return fire, Everett despatched the last of his ammunition into the Condor and saw it burst into flames, plunging into the sea. Everett then managed to coax the Hurricat to about 2,000 feet (610 m), despite the damage. He landed the plane in the water near the destroyer HMS *Wanderer*, which was assigned to a neighbouring convoy.

As he ditched into the sea – an extremely perilous task – the plane turned over and sank as soon as it touched the water, dragging him down 30 feet (9 m). Incredibly, he managed to struggle free and was picked up by another destroyer in his convoy. For his skill and courage he was awarded the DSO in September 1941.

Everett was killed, flying a Hurricane from Belfast to Abingdon when it came down in shallow waters close to the beach at Llanddona, Anglesey, on 26 January 1942. Possibly he'd had engine problems. The wreck of his plane was soon recovered, but his body was only washed ashore several months later. A post-mortem revealed he had drowned.

He is buried close to the crash scene in St Dona's Church, Llanddona.

## A FURIOUS ATTACK IN THE ARCTIC

Another lesser-known but equally heroic RAF Hurricat fighter pilot aboard a CAM ship was South African Alistair Hay, DFC (1921–44). He had enlisted in the RAF as a volunteer reservist in 1942 and with his strong nautical background was rapidly promoted to Flight Lieutenant.

On 27 May 1942, he was aboard the Hurricat CAM ship HMS *Empire Lawrence*, part of an Arctic convoy in the freezing waters near Murmansk, when the convoy was attacked by German seaplanes. To counter the attack he jumped into his Sea Hurricane and, after being blasted off the ship, took on the approaching formation of German aircraft. The furious torpedo attack came from six German Heinkel He 111 and Junkers Ju 88 adapted seaplanes for long-range patrolling.

The odds against the young man were perilously high – six against one. He came under extreme fire, was severely wounded – shot in the thigh – and was bleeding heavily as he managed to bail out. But he had destroyed one German aircraft and damaged another.

The convoy escort ship, HMS *Volunteer*, spotted his parachute and Hay was picked up from the icy waters in an equally dramatic rescue operation, the ship coming under heavy fire from torpedo bombers as Alistair Hay was hoisted aboard.

Hay's DFC citation, awarded on 23 June 1942, read: 'He showed great gallantry and his spirited attack was a great encouragement to all the convoy and escorts and cannot but have been a great discomfort and surprise to the enemy.'

Recovering from his wounds, Hay later joined 182 Squadron, flying a fighter-bomber Typhoon IB, accompanying the Allied advance through France and Holland after the D-Day landings on 6 June.

On 18 August 1944, he was shot down encountering flak near Vimoutiers, north-west France. He is buried in Calvados, near Caen.

From August 1941 to July 1943 a total of nine of these sea combat launches resulted in the destruction of nine German aircraft (four Condors, four Heinkel 111s and a Junkers Ju 88) with one damaged. Eight Hurricanes were ditched and one pilot was lost.

The CAM vessels were phased out from mid-1942 due to the arrival of Merchant Aircraft Carriers. These could carry Hurricanes that had undergone minor conversions to operate at sea.

The first Sea Hurricanes – Mark IBs – went into service in July 1941 and other versions followed in 1942, including the Mark IC (with four cannon) and the Mark IIC (equipped with naval radio gear).

The Sea Hurricane remained in service until 1943, then it was deployed in a range of theatres, including Russia and the

ABOVE: US and British members of the Air Transport Auxilary ready to take up Hurricane fighter planes for delivery to RAF pilots, June 1942.

LEFT: Two of the first American women to join the ATA, Virginia Farr and Louise Schuurman, seen here with a Hurricane fighter ready for delivery to the RAF, at an airfield 'somewhere In England'.

RIGHT: A pilot of No. 6 Squadron stands by his Hawker Hurricane Mark IID at Shandur, Egypt. This view shows the 40mm Vickers anti-tank cannon, which the squadron used to good effect in the fighting in North Africa.

CENTRE: Hawker Hurricane Mark IIDs of No. 6 Squadron taking off in Tunisia soon after noon on 6 April 1943 for a tank-busting raid.

RIGHT: Squadron Leader R R Stanford-Tuck, Commanding Officer of No. 257 Squadron RAF, sitting in the cockpit of his Hawker Hurricane Mark I, V6864 'DT-A', at Coltishall, Norfolk. The Burmese flag is seen painted on the starboard side of the aircraft and on the port side were painted 26 victory symbols, c. 1941.

ABOVE: A Hawker Hurricane Mark IV of No. 6 Squadron RAF being serviced on an airfield in Italy, prior to a sortie over the Adriatic, July 1944.

BELOW: Pilot Officer A V 'Taffy' Clowes of No. 1 Squadron RAF, standing by his Hawker Hurricane Mark I, October 1940. The wasp emblem was painted on the nose of his aircraft during the Battle of Britain, Clowes adding a new stripe to the body for each enemy aircraft he shot down. His final score was at least twelve.

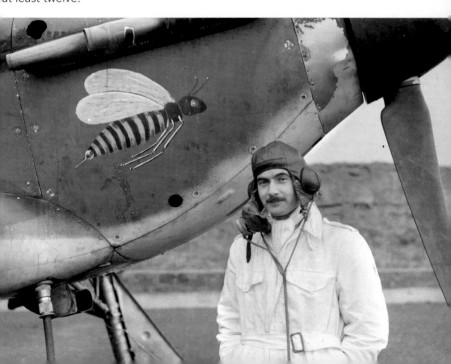

ABOVE: Squadron Leader Marmaduke Thomas St John 'Pat' Pattle, Officer Commanding No. 33 Squadron RAF, and the Squadron Adjutant, Flight Lieutenant George Rumsey, standing by a Hawker Hurricane at Larissa, Thessaly, Greece. This photo was taken in March–April 1941, shortly before Pat was shot down in the Battle of Athens.

LEFT: War correspondent Ernest Hemingway walks a London street in the company of RAF Officer Roald Dahl of 80 Squadron, 1944.

RIGHT: Pilots of 32 Squadron at Biggin Hill, Kent, England in July 1940, relaxing shortly before the opening shots of the Battle of Britain. Behind them a Hawker Hurricane single-seat fighter aircraft.

RIGHT AND BELOW: A letter written by a Flight Lieutenant, Thomas Gilbert Pace, in November 1940 to a Canadian girl, recounting his experiences since he had been posted with No. 85 Fighter Squadron to France. He describes in vivid detail his first encounters with enemy bombers on 10 May and his crash landing the following day after his Hurricane was damaged by a Heinkel.

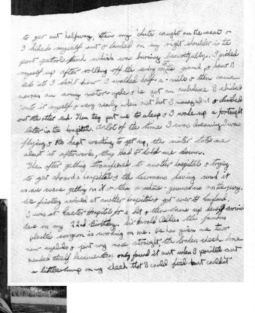

ABOVE: Pilots of No. 303 Polish Fighter Squadron gathering around the inscribed tail-fin of their 178th victim, a Junkers Ju 88, at RAF Kirton-in-Lindsey, August 1942. Among them is Flight Sergeant Kazimierz Wünsche (far right of the second picture).

LEFT: Wünsche playing with Misia, the Squadron's dog-mascot, at RAF Kirton-in-Lindsey, August 1942.

BELOW: The family of Sergeant Wünsche seen proudly alongside the remains of the Hurricane he flew during the Battle of Britain. Miraculously Wünsche survived the crash. (Operation Nightingale excavation of Hurricane P3700 in 2015.)

ABOVE AND BELOW: RAF veteran Jeff Brereton of 605 Squadron and later 32 Squadron visits Duxford Airfield. Pictured here with a Hawker Hurricane Mk 1 R4118 and Hurricane Heritage pilot James Brown.

ABOVE: The Hawker Hurricane P3717 was flying with 253 Squadron during the Battle of Britain and was involved in various encounters with the Luftwaffe. It was eventually sent to Russia from where its remains were retrieved for restoration back to flight.

BELOW: As the 'Last of the Many', Hawker Hurricane PZ865 was the last off the production line. It is painted to represent a 247 Squadron Night Fighter and it belongs to the Royal Air Force, Battle of Britain Memorial Flight. It is based at RAF Coningsby, Lincolnshire.

Mediterranean, yet it was not entirely suitable for maritime work, due to its size, slow climb and poor ditching qualities in the water.

Through the war, around 500 Sea Hurricanes served with the Fleet Air Arm and an estimated 1,200 Hurricanes were converted for maritime use. In April 1944, the last Sea Hurricane was removed from carrier service.

# CHAPTER 5

# A GLOBAL ENTERPRISE

Tʜᴇ Hᴜʀʀɪᴄᴀɴᴇ ɪs ʙᴇsᴛ ʀᴇᴍᴇᴍʙᴇʀᴇᴅ ᴀs an interceptor fighter in the Battle of Britain. Yet afterwards it fulfilled many different roles. Robust, capable of withstanding rough treatment in climates around the world, it continued to operate in key wartime theatres.

## THE BATTLE FOR MALTA
## (10 JUNE 1940–20 NOVEMBER 1942)

Through the years from 1940 to 1942, the tiny Mediterranean island of Malta, then a British Crown Colony, became one of the most bombed places in the world.

The battle for this island, a maritime base of paramount strategic importance to the Allies and Axis powers alike, turned out to be one of the most decisive turning points of the Second World War.

Against huge odds, the RAF turned almost certain defeat into aerial triumph in a battle since acknowledged as key to the Allied victory in North Africa – and the subsequent Allied invasion of southern Europe.

As soon as Mussolini declared war on Britain and France on 10 June 1940, Malta went on alert. The first air raid on the island took place the following day when Italian bombers, SM.79 Sparvieros (Italian for sparrowhawk), attacked Malta's Grand Harbour, Halfar and Kalafrana. Malta's air defence initially involved obsolescent Gloster Sea Gladiators.

Before the end of June, four Hurricanes – already en route to Egypt – were diverted to the defence of Malta. In July, when one Hurricane and one Gladiator were already lost, Hurricanes at the RAF Luqa airfield were to prove central in Malta's survival. The plane was capable of dealing with the Italian SM 79 bomber. But more fighters were desperately needed.

On 24 July 1940, the reconditioned aircraft carrier HMS Argus left Liverpool, England, with twelve Hurricanes. Argus was supported by a strong escorting force, including the battlecruiser Hood, two battleships, aircraft carrier Ark Royal, two cruisers and ten destroyers.

On 2 August, the Hurricanes were successfully flown off the carrier into Malta. Ground staff were landed by submarine or via Sunderland flying boat under cover of night.

By 13 October, Winston Churchill had fully acknowledged the perilous state of Malta's defences. 'First in urgency is the reinforcement of Malta – by further Hurricane aircraft flown there as best can be managed.'

Yet a Hurricane reinforcement operation on 17 November via HMS Argus ended badly. Fourteen fighters took off into a headwind too far from the island and only five landed safely. Nine ran out of petrol and were lost.

By the end of 1940, fourteen Hurricanes were on Malta. Then the German forces commenced their attack on the island. The first of the Luftwaffe to arrive in the Mediterranean was Fliegerkorps X, a coastal air corps. It arrived in nearby

Sicily in January 1941. The aim was to attack Malta and its shipping, assisted by the Italian Regia Aeronautica (the Italian Royal Air Force). In the months that followed, Malta remained under sustained bombardment from 350 aircraft of the Fliegerkorps X.

By mid-January 1941, an Allied convoy, led by HMS *Illustrious*, was constantly being attacked by air as it made its way into Valletta's Grand Harbour.

Badly damaged, with 126 crew killed and 91 wounded, the *Illustrious* was still able to dock, unload and, on 23 January, set sail again for Alexandria to deliver supplies, thanks to the heroic efforts of ship repairers, naval teams and the RAF. The Hurricanes, aided by a massive anti-aircraft barrage from the Maltese ground defences, put up a determined fight against the German onslaught. At the end of January, 6 more Hurricanes arrived in Malta from the Middle East.

Yet as the raids on Malta continued, the casualties from Hurricanes (Mark I and Mark II) were increasing. The Me 109s were proving formidable opponents. In February 1941, an attack on Malta shot down 2 Hurricanes. By late spring, the Luftwaffe's Fliegerkorps X was moved east to Greece and Crete.

On 27 April, 23 Hurricanes (6 Mark Is) were delivered to Malta from carrier HMS *Ark Royal*. The delivery, despite bad weather causing take-off to be postponed, succeeded – in the midst of attacks from Me 109s and Ju 88s.

A further 45 Hurricane Mark IIAs were delivered to Malta in May/June 1941, flown off the aircraft carriers HMS *Ark Royal* and HMS *Victorious* as part of Operation Rocket. Similar operations on 27 and 30 June brought another 64 fighters to the island, though some were moved on to Egypt.

Tom Neil, of 249 Squadron, whose experiences in the Battle

of Britain were recounted in Chapter 4, was co-leading the Hurricane's flight off the carrier HMS *Ark Royal*. He would remain in Malta until November 1941. His time there, flying the Hurricane in a series of hazardous sorties, was later documented in his memoir *Onward to Malta*.

## FIRST FLIGHT INTO MALTA

It was 21 May 1941. As he climbed into his Hurricane Mark I that day, Tom Neil was well aware that the Hurricane mission to Malta would prove difficult. Boxes were being used to store the pilot's gear – the aircraft had no extra cockpit space even for baggage.

> 'We had to take off at dawn, just about in the dark, and our squadron, 249, was going to be split into two; the squadron commander was going to take the first twelve because by that time I was senior flight commander, aged twenty, and I was going to lead the second group of eleven aircraft.'

Take-off from the *Ark Royal* carrier went without a hitch. But just as Neil started to climb away from the vessel, he heard a loud bang. The aircraft dropped a wing and started flying sideways in an alarming fashion.

A gun panel had become loose. It seemed as if the Hurricane would be heading into the sea, but fortunately Neil managed to bring it under control.

He considered landing back on the *Ark Royal*, but this was too dangerous, given the damage to the plane. He decided to fly on, but after about an hour, the guiding Fairey Fulmar (a Fleet

Air Arm convoy used for Malta) had mysteriously disappeared from the sky before him.

Later, it turned out that an engine pipe on the Fulmar had burst, leaving its windscreen covered in black oil, so the pilot had dived away to return to the carrier.

This was bewildering. Without any maps, Neil was lost. Worse, the other Hurricanes were dependent on him. He broke radio silence, spoke to the other airmen.

No one had any idea how to reach Malta. They'd been in the air for two hours by then. The Hurricanes could be at the limit of their power by the time they reached Malta.

The flight continued. The time passed. The needle on Neil's petrol gauge sank lower. The horizon stretched ahead. Then, with very few gallons to spare, Malta appeared below 'with magical suddenness'.

Overwhelmed with relief, Tom Neil came down in a cloud of dust at Luqa – in the middle of an air raid. But they'd survived. He recalled later:

> 'We'd been airborne for five hours and twenty-five minutes, probably the longest operational trip ever made by a Hurricane.'

The Hurricane reinforcements helped Malta in the summer and the second half of 1941: German raids diminished when the Luftwaffe units moved away to Russia. More Hurricanes arrived in late June, including four-cannon Mark IICs, which went to squadrons 126 and 185.

On 30 June, 126 Squadron shot down two Macchi MC 200 fighters. On 4 July, 185 Squadron had its first fight on cannon-armed Hurricanes, destroying two Macchis and damaging three, without losses.

Recalled Graham Leggett, who had joined 249 Squadron in late June:

> 'There did not appear to be much enemy activity at the time. What we had was a private war between three squadrons of Hurricanes and the Italian air force in Sicily, which was very much a comic opera. The Luftwaffe had been in Sicily in considerable strength but had then been sent to the Russian front. The Italians were not really interested in this war. They did not bother us much.'

The ensuing months saw only desultory enemy raids: 185 Squadron claimed eight more Italian warplanes in July, and No. 126 Squadron downed four Macchi MC 200s on 19 August, and three more on 4 September.

Yet the Hurricanes had losses too: Pilot Officer David Usher Barnwell (1921–41) had recently received a DFC for destroying five Italian aircraft in one week. He was shot down and crashed into the sea on 14 October, aged nineteen. His body was never found.

For Tom Neil, the quality of the Hurricanes he flew was troubling. In his first eight weeks, he had five engine failures. He'd frequently sit there during take-off feeling apprehensive, waiting for loss of power or stoppage.

The Mark II arrival didn't assuage his feelings. The versions his squadron received for Malta had not been tropicalized, so 'they managed to suck in every article of dust and filth whipped up by our whirling airscrews'.

Neil believed that Malta needed more Spitfires, faster in combat. But so long as the RAF's domestic fighter force maintained vast numbers of Supermarine and Hawker fighters at home – believing that the Germans might renew their daylight offensive – despatching other fighters to overseas theatres like Malta remained unlikely. It was felt that the Hurricane Mark II would be sufficient – and anyway, the Spitfire was far less robust than the Hurricane.

By the end of November 1941, as German fighter bombers in Sicily made ready for an extensive attack, determined to seize Malta and secure the all-important sea route towards North Africa, the clouds of war over Malta grew ever darker.

Prior to this, more Hurricanes had arrived on Malta. Forty-nine reached the island at various times from aircraft carriers HMS *Ark Royal* and HMS *Furious*. On 12 November, twenty-one Mark IIBs of 242 Squadron and sixteen more from 605 Squadron flew off the two carriers. This would be the last journey, however, of the 'Ark', previously considered a 'lucky ship'. The following day, the carrier was sunk by a U-boat on returning from Gibraltar.

Now there remained just three squadrons of Hurricanes ready to meet any renewed German assault on Malta. The Junkers Ju 88s were escorted by the improved Messerschmitt Bf 109Fs. It became hugely difficult for the Hurricanes to engage them, given their slow rate of climb.


## THE MALTA BATTLE WORSENS

Through the last week of December 1941 and into January 1942, the Hurricanes were still succeeding in breaking up enemy formations. But as the German offensive on Malta developed even further in February, the situation worsened dramatically.

February 1942 saw 222 raids on Malta's airfields. Heavy rain made matters worse. Thanks to a huge effort from ground crews, soldiers and civilians, the runways remained in operation and the Hurricanes continued to take off. But by then, life was increasingly tough for the RAF fighters. At the beginning of February, twenty-eight Hurricanes were serviceable. By the 15 February, there were just eleven.

However, in January 1942, the inadequacy of the defending fighters on Malta had finally been acknowledged following a report from a senior RAF Commander, Group Captain Basil Embry (later Air Chief Marshal), who had visited Valletta. His report made it very clear that the Messerschmitt Bf 109F was now superior in every respect to the Hurricane Mark II.

'The morale of the pilots seems to be high although the obsolescent Hurricane IIs are having a certain effect on the pilots. I am informed that the German fighter pilots often fly in front of our Hurricanes in order to show off the superiority of the Bf 109Fs. This is bound to have an increasingly adverse effect on the morale of the pilots. I therefore consider that every possible step should be taken to make Spitfire Vs and Kittyhawks available with the least delay.'

(The Kittyhawk was a development of the monoplane Curtiss Hawk fighter, an American designed and built fighter providing the RAF with reinforcements in the Middle East in 1941/2.)

On 25 January 1942, the validity of his report was underlined, as nineteen Hurricane IIs from Squadrons 249, 242, 185 and 126 scrambled to intercept an incoming raid in clear skies. Labouring to gain height to meet the marauders, the pilots were bounced by the 109s, which swept in high and fast, four aircraft line abreast – with disastrous results. Of the nineteen Hurricanes, seven were shot down, three returned early with mechanical trouble. Four pilots had bailed out, two had crash-landed and one was shot down into the sea with the pilot killed. A third of Malta's defenders had been wiped out – and a quarter of all serviceable fighters on Malta destroyed.

By early March 1942 – with the Germans flying six hundred sorties to Malta each week – just twelve Hurricanes were operational. Effectively, the Hurricanes had been all but obliterated. So severe were the shortages that some of the pilots of 249 Squadron were reduced to standing on the rooftops of Valletta to act as plane spotters.

In late February 1942, Squadron Leader Stan Turner, DFC and Bar, a Canadian Battle of Britain veteran, then the Commanding Officer of 249 Squadron on Malta, told the AOC Air Vice Marshal Hugh Lloyd: 'Either, sir, we get Spitfires here within days, not weeks, or we're done. That's it.'

## WILL A NEW FIGHTER MAKE A DIFFERENCE?

On 7 March, fifteen new fighters flew in to Malta from the aircraft carrier HMS *Eagle*. Here were the Mark Vb Spitfires, the first to operate outside Britain. Sixteen more arrived later that month.

Graham Leggett, with 249 Squadron, witnessed the relief that surged through the Maltese people at the arrival of the new fighters.

'The Maltese practically went mad. They knew the score. They knew the Hurricanes were having a tough time against the 109s. We were losing a lot of planes and a lot of people.'

No. 249 Squadron, already credited with around twenty victories for Hurricanes, was then converted to Spitfires, followed by 126 Squadron, whose Hurricanes had been credited with destroying thirty-four enemy planes – with a loss of ten of their number.

The Spitfire Vb's higher rate of climb meant they were, indeed, better able to tackle the raiders. But after their arrival, aircraft shortages still continued to be a problem, given the more fragile nature of the Spit.

Less robust than the Hurricanes, by mid-April virtually all the new Spitfires became unserviceable, mostly because of incessant attacks on the airfields. German raids on Malta in March 1942 had doubled those of the previous month.

By mid-March, serviceable Hurricanes increased to thirty. They were still operated by 185 Squadron, and on the 21 March a decisive victory was achieved: four Hurricanes attacked eight Bf 100s that were strafing the newly built RAF Takali airfield, afterwards claiming to have shot down six.

On 27 March, ten Hurricane IICs of 229 Squadron arrived from North Africa, and another fifteen arrived in April, taking over the Hurricanes previously flown by Squadrons 126 or 249.

## A CHANGE OF FORTUNE

The assault from the air on Malta had become a shocking ordeal for its 250,000 inhabitants, living through the continuous bombing, struggling to survive as the lack of food and medicine overwhelmed the ravaged island.

On 15 April, the people of Malta were awarded the George Cross in recognition of their heroic struggle against the incessant attacks on the island.

Thankfully, further Spitfires were on their way aboard the American fleet carrier, *Wasp*. With its long flight deck, *Wasp* could carry greater numbers.

On 20 April, forty-seven Spitfires flew off the carrier heading for two bases on Malta. Yet again, the enemy relentlessly pounced on them. The following day, just seventeen of the new Spitfires were serviceable. Within three days, every single one was grounded. For five days in April there was just one Spitfire available to defend the island.

By now, the Allies were totally focused on deploying their RAF resources to the island. Allied fortunes in the air seemed to be hanging by less than a thread as the Hurricane struggled to defend Malta.

For a newly arrived squadron on the island, viewing the skies above Malta was a painful sight.

Squadron Leader Percy Belgrave Lucas – usually known as Laddie Lucas – joined the RAF in 1940 and arrived in Malta on 17 February 1942. He would soon take command of 249 Squadron. What he saw on his arrival was a shocking confirmation of the desperately urgent need for more, better fighters.

'A strung-out antiquated VIC [a formation of fighters resembling the letter V] of five Hurricanes breathlessly clambering to gain height, heading south-east in a palpably forlorn quest to achieve some sort of position to strike at the incoming raid.

'High above, three sections of four Me 109Fs in open line abreast formation were racing at will across the powdered sky spelling out a message of unmistakable supremacy.'

Yet the Hurricane's determined resistance – echoing the story of the Battle of Britain, where the fighters somehow held off for just enough time – would now witness a change in Malta's fortunes.

Demands from Hitler's forces in Russia and North Africa meant that German aircraft resources were miraculously diverted elsewhere. On 30 April, only the Italian bombers were attacking Malta: bomber losses for the Italians and Germans had now become alarmingly high.

Malta's ordeal did not end there. But the Allied fighters could now re-equip. The diversion of the Luftwaffe's effort from Sicily to North Africa and the arrival of greater numbers of Spitfires set a pattern that would gradually ease the situation considerably.

The Hurricane's struggle had made a significant contribution to the battle for Malta. But by July 1942, the last remaining Hurricanes on the island were pulled out of the front line. Some Mark Is were sent to the Middle East, others were retained for night fighting.


## THE BATTLE FINALLY ENDS

Eighty-five Spitfires arrived in Malta in August and October: during that month the Luftwaffe renewed its attacks on the island. But by the end of October, the Luftwaffe offensive ended: early November brought news of the Allies' rapid advances in North Africa at El Alamein.

Two supply convoys with cargoes of food and essential provisions reached Malta in November and December unscathed. By the end of 1942, supply ships could now arrive in Malta without accompanying convoys, and on 20

November 1942 the battle for Malta ended, though it would be several months before the deprivations of the Maltese people finally ceased.

Diversion of the Luftwaffe's main effort from Sicily to North Africa and the arrival of yet more Spitfires ultimately helped secure Malta's safety from invasion. But without the Hurricane's earlier commitment there would have been no battle left to fight in 1942. It had made a real contribution to the island's survival. Had Malta fallen, Britain's triumph at El Alamein at the end of 1942 could not have been achieved.

## THE HURRI AND THE SOVIET UNION

On 22 June 1941, Nazi Germany launched a surprise attack against the Soviet Union, its ally in 1939. By the end of 1941, German troops had advanced hundreds of miles to the outskirts of Moscow.

Known as Operation Barbarossa, the German invasion into the Soviet Union became one of the largest military operations in the history of modern warfare. More than three and a half million troops were assembled for Germany's attack, supported by the Luftwaffe, artillery and tanks.

On 12 July 1941, an Anglo-Soviet Agreement was signed in Moscow between Britain and the Russians, a military alliance to fight together against Nazi Germany.

Enter the Hurricane. By March that year, Hurricane production had reached close to a hundred a week. Thanks to the UK's Anglo-Soviet Agreement and the Lend Lease Act, the Kremlin, acutely aware that the Soviet air force urgently needed more fighters, requested three thousand more fighters for delivery to the Soviet Union. (The Lend Lease Act – enacted in March 1941 – was a policy under which the US supplied the United Kingdom, the Soviet Union and other Allied countries with food, oil and other material, including warships, war planes and weapons. It proved to be a vital resource for the Soviets until it ended in September 1945.)

Churchill had promised that Hurricanes would be handed over to Soviet pilots if they 'could use them effectively'.

The Hurri became the first Western Allied fighter aircraft to arrive in the Soviet Union, deployed on the Eastern Front. It would also fly air defence missions around the warm-water port of Murmansk.

The first twenty four-cannon-equipped Hurricane IIBs arrived north-east of Murmansk on 7 September 1941 via seaborne supply convoys sailing within range of Luftwaffe attacks launched from Norway and Finland. Merchant ships then transported another fifteen boxed Hurricanes and ground equipment to the northern port of Archangel where the thirty-nine Hurri fighter planes were then assembled. Two accompanying RAF Hurricane squadrons, 81 and 134 Squadron, were tasked primarily to train Soviet pilots to fly the Hurricane after delivery to the Soviet Union – and to patrol the skies above Murmansk.

This was the first 'batch' of Hurricanes to be sent to the Soviet Union. The ground crews accompanying the two squadrons – mostly British, Australian and New Zealanders – were experienced: many were Battle of Britain veterans.

Throughout their time in Murmansk and Archangel, the RAF squadrons continued to fly air patrols over the area, holding off enemy Luftwaffe forces from Murmansk and providing cover to Soviet troops. In one battle, 81 Squadron shot down three Bf 109 escorts: one Hurricane was lost and one pilot killed.

## TEACHING THE RUSSIANS TO FLY A HURRI

On 15 September 1940, Flight Lieutenant Ray Holmes was flying a Hurricane over south-east London when he spotted a formation of German Dornier Do 17 bombers heading for central London. He successfully rammed one of the German aircraft and managed to survive by parachuting out of his Hurricane as the stricken German aircraft spiralled onto the forecourt of London's Victoria Station. Fêted by an overenthusiastic press at the time as a Battle of Britain hero who had 'saved' Buckingham Palace it was, without question, a truly heroic act – but many years later it became regarded as a much disputed legend.

Ray continued to fly for the RAF throughout the war. In June 1941, he joined 81 Squadron as they set off overseas. (During the war, any overseas destination of troops and RAF personnel was described as 'destination unknown' for security reasons.) In this case, the journey ahead was a highly risky undertaking – a maritime journey heading towards the Soviet Union, now at war with Germany. The German air threat to Arctic convoys like these made for a very dangerous journey and it took Ray's squadron nearly three months through icy and perilous waters until the aircraft carrier HMS *Argus*, carrying twenty-four Hurricane IIBs, arrived at the Soviet Varenga airfield, a few miles north-east of Murmansk.

The RAF squadrons were there to teach the Soviet pilots how to fly the Hurricane Mark IIBs. One by one, the Russian pilots took their first solo flights on Hurricanes. 'They had posted some of their most experienced flyers to Murmansk to fly the nucleus of the first Soviet Hurricane squadrons – and these boys were not slow to tell us how good they were,' recalled Ray.

The Soviet pilots had been flying Ilyushin 1-16s, a sturdy, stubby-winged monoplane which they assured the RAF men were very difficult to fly. A pilot who could fly one of these, they claimed, could fly anything. Ray and his colleagues assured the Soviet pilots that the Hurricanes had no vice and that any fool could fly them.

> 'After they had bent one or two Hurricanes by heavy landings, and we had reminded them that "only the best pilots can fly the I-16", our message went home and they started to take more notice of what we had told them.'

Towards the end of their time there, the RAF men handed over much of their equipment to the Russians.

> 'The agreement was that we were to leave them everything, taking nothing home but personal belongings. Lorries, petrol tankers, vans disappeared. Flying helmets, goggles, headphones and Mae Wests (inflatable life jackets) went too.'

Given the freezing temperatures and snow throughout most of their time there, the RAF men were allowed to keep their wool-lined flying boots for warmth. As identification they kept a folded Union Jack in a plastic holder – to be whipped out and waved if they were shot down and had to make their way back through Russian lines.

The RAF handover was completed by the end of October and the squadrons returned home in December. By the end of 1941, one hundred Hurricanes had reached the Soviet Union.

By the time of the RAF's departure, three Soviet squadrons

had been successfully converted to Hurricanes. Flying the twelve-gun Hurricane IIBs, Soviet pilots from Murmansk were credited with shooting down fifteen Luftwaffe German aircraft – with the loss of just one Hurricane. By the end of 1941, a hundred Hurricanes had reached the Soviet Union.

Through the winter of 1941 and 1942, the Soviet Hurricanes suffered heavy losses against the highly trained Luftwaffe pilots. From Murmansk in the far north to Stalingrad in the south, Hurricanes were used against the invading German forces.

Essentially, the Soviet pilots were 'earning their stripes' in the Hurricane. Eventually, they were able to transition to newly arrived US fighters, the P-39s and P-40s, and later on, to more advanced Soviet-built fighters.

In the years between 1941 and 1944, a total of 2,950 Hurricanes from British and Canadian production were sent to the Soviet Union. These were used in a variety of roles, from air defence interceptor to ground-attack aircraft and spotter. As the US Lend Lease deliveries continued and Soviet aviation began to maintain a more active front in the east, the Hurricanes were gradually relegated to secondary duties.

## THE SOVIET HURRICANES

The Hurricanes sent to the Soviet Union from British and Canadian production included 1,557 Hurricane Mark IIBs, 210 Hurricane Mark IIAs (some with Mark I conversions), 1,009 Hurricane Mark IICs, 60 tank-busting Mark IIDs and an estimated 100 Hurricane Mark IVs. Some were later adapted by the Russians to carry American 0.5-inch (12.7-mm) machine guns; four two-seaters were produced, two modified as two-seater trainers by the Russians in 1946, and two four-seaters built at Hawker with Mark IICs.

The Hurricanes were not the most popular fighter in the Soviet Union. Soviet aviation specialists were able to examine the Hawker Hurricane for the first time when a Soviet delegation visiting Germany (in the months before Germany invaded the Soviet Union) was given the opportunity to examine several aircraft captured by Germany. These included the Hawker Hurricane and the Supermarine Spitfire. The delegation was reported to have noted that the Hurricane was obsolete when compared to the Spitfire. Spitfires were deemed to be a better military proposition.

Some accounts claimed the Soviets were furious at not receiving more Spitfires, just part-worn Hurricanes. (They'd already received one hundred and fifty Spitfires.) Yet by sending large quantities of P-39s, P-40s and Spitfires the Western allies gave the Soviet pilots the tools they needed to fight the Luftwaffe – and win. Moreover, the arrival of the aid from the Western Allies gave Soviet engineers time to develop effective aircraft of their own – in large numbers.

Some surviving Hurricanes remained on Russian territory after the Second World War ended. There were reports that, because Stalin did not want his people to know about the aid from their former Allies, the British planes were dropped down empty mineshafts.

The Hurricane's contribution to the Second World War history of the Soviet Union was overshadowed by that of the Spitfire. Yet given those months of 1941 and early 1942, when the Hurricane helped the Soviet military hold the line against the Germans in the important port of Murmansk, it remains a worthy contributor to the story.

## THE DESERT WAR: THE NORTH AFRICA
## CAMPAIGN (10 JUNE 1940-13 MAY 1943)

The North Africa campaign was the last great offensive against Germany in which the Hurricanes participated in any significant numbers.

Fighting between the Allies and the Axis powers had started with Italy's declaration of war in June 1940. The German Afrika Korps commanded by Field Marshal Erwin Rommel – 'The Desert Fox' – one of Hitler's favourite generals, arrived in North Africa in February 1941. Primarily a 'blocking force' to Libya to support the Italian Army, a series of battles for control of Libya and Egypt followed.

The conflict reached a climax in the Battle of El Alamein when Allied forces, under the command of Lieutenant General Bernard Montgomery, inflicted a decisive defeat on Rommel's Afrika Korps, pushing its remaining forces into Tunisia. In May 1943, Allied forces then forced the surrender of several hundred thousand Germans and Italians in northern Tunisia.

It was in North Africa's Western Desert that the Hurricane 'tank buster' entered the Second World War. The Allies had fought through to Egypt with the aim of stopping Rommel's drive in the desert to seize Egypt and the Suez Canal, Britain's lifeline in the area.

With its flat open expanses, North Africa's Western Desert was the ideal arena for tanks, affording them speed and manoeuvrability. The Allies needed the right aircraft to take them on. Though the Hurricane was able to strafe German troops, its bombing efforts thus far had been wildly inaccurate, pretty much hit and miss.

What was needed was ground-attack aircraft fitted with anti-tank guns. Destroying German tanks was difficult; bombing them was almost impossible. Could the development of a tank buster be the answer?

## THE TANK BUSTER

This idea had been conceived as far back as 1939, when manufacturers had started to work on the development of 40-mm (1.6-in) armour-piercing cannon in aircraft for use against tanks. RAF top brasses originally believed that tanks should be defeated by tanks, not airborne fighters.

In May 1941, Hawker Aircraft were asked to investigate the possibility of fitting tank-busting weapons under each wing of the Hurricane Mark II. And on 18 September, Hawker test pilot Kenneth Seth-Smith test-flew a Mark IIB Z2326 armed with two Vickers Type 'S' 40-mm anti-tank guns.

The trial proved satisfactory. Enter the Hurricane Mark IID, which would become known eventually as a 'tank buster'.

A new-build version, which started the following year, added armour to protect the cockpit, radiator and engine from ground fire. Like other Mark IIs, it had a Merlin XX engine armed with a pair of 40-mm Vickers 'S' anti-tank guns and a single 0.303-inch (7.7-mm) machine gun to assist with aiming. It retained two wing-mounted Browning 0.303-inch machine guns, but these normally fired tracer ammunition.

To aid sighting the two 40-mm cannon, either a Vickers Type 'S' or Rolls-Royce BF (belt feed) could be used. The former was preferred because it carried fifteen rounds per gun, compared with twelve rounds on the Rolls-Royce version. The 'S' cannons were sighted through a conventional Mark II reflex sight; in addition, the aircraft carried two Browning 0.5 sighting machine guns loaded with tracers (bullets or projectiles). Top speed of the aircraft, fully loaded, was 304 mph (489 km/h), but when the IID was fitted with a tropical filter beneath the nose, as most were, speed declined to 288 mph (463 km/h).

From December 1942, 184 Squadron flew IIDs – but did not enter combat with them. They were confined to training exercises with the army. The majority of IIDs were shipped overseas, including to 6 Squadron, stationed in Egypt. (The squadron spent its entire time throughout the Second World War in the Mediterranean.) No. 6 Squadron were the first to fly the new IIDs, which arrived in April 1942. The squadron had previously flown Hurricane Mark Is to operate with the 2nd Armoured Division in Egypt.

At Shandur, Egypt, over the Suez Canal, intensive training runs of the new IIDs were carried out, including live firing of captured enemy tanks. The training revealed that while the recoil of the guns tended to pitch the Hurricane's nose down – so that fresh aim had to be taken – it was still possible to fire the next salvo almost immediately.

Squadron Leader Donald Weston-Burt, DSO, was positive about this:

'If the IID fired its first pair of 40-mms at 1,000 yards [914 m], two more pairs could be got away accurately before breaking off the attack.

'It is no exaggeration to say that any good pilot could guarantee to hit his target with one or more pairs on each attack.'

The training was completed on 4 June and the squadron moved to Gambut in Libya, where Axis forces under Rommel had just started their offensive.

No. 6 Squadron's first mission with the tank buster on 7 June was aborted. But on the following day, an attack on an enemy convoy west of Bir Hakeim left two German tanks and a couple of trucks destroyed.

A further sortie on the same day took place when Flight Lieutenant Alan Simpson, a Canadian flying BN861, continued with his quick-firing mobile anti-tank gun attack on a German Mark III tank – despite already being severely wounded in the chest.

> 'My initial reaction was to cost the enemy as much as possible so I lined up on another and then a truck.'

He then flew blind for some time before bailing out at 500 feet (152 m). He was picked up and returned to his unit three months later after recovering. Subsequently, he was awarded a DFC.

This was the beginning 6 Squadron's period of hectic action up to and just after El Alamein.

On 24 October, 6 Squadron IIDs scored sixteen tanks. The following month, the squadron was held off operations and began convoy patrols off Alexandria with Hurricane IICs – they were also responsible for training other squadrons on the IIDs. The squadron returned to tank busting in March 1943.

## THE FLYING TIN OPENERS

The tank-busting IIDs claimed at least fifty Axis tanks and large numbers of armoured vehicles, as well as destroying field guns, trucks and other transport. The low-level successful attacks against enemy armour earned 6 Squadron its nickname, 'The Flying Tin Openers': an emblem symbolizing the tin openers was carried on 6 Squadron aircraft afterwards.

No. 6 Squadron's IIDs played a full part in the El Alamein offensive, exacting a heavy toll on Rommel's armour and support vehicles, although there were numerous Hurricane losses.

In many ways, the IID, the first-ever tank buster, was a pioneer, the great-grandfather of today's US A10 'Warthog', a flying gun and tank buster.

Beyond the success of the El Alamein offensive, two other RAF squadrons equipped with tank busters flew in the North-West Frontier – the region then part of the British Indian Empire (now Pakistan).

No. 5 Squadron flew the IID as a bomber escort and in ground-attack missions from June to December 1943 while the squadron was based at RAF Kharagpur, West Bengal. In June 1944, the IID was replaced by the US P-47 Thunderbolt, a fast fighter-bomber and ground-attack aircraft that the squadron retained until March 1946.

No. 20 Squadron flew the IID from March 1943 to September 1945. In that period, the IIDs were moved to north-west Burma – they were the only squadron in the area equipped with the flying tin openers – targeting enemy armour as well as attacking lines of communication, i.e. river boats and trucks (see Chapter 6). In the last months of 1944, 20 Squadron undertook aerial spraying with their tank busters (to minimize the spread of malaria).

(In December 1944, 20 Squadron converted to the rocket-projectile Hurricane IV during the Allied advance towards Rangoon – and the Allied capture of Burma in May 1945.)

## THE BATTLE OF ATHENS

Aside from the Hurricane's role in Allied support for the Soviet Union and its courageous battles in Malta and the North African desert, its other roles in the global conflict should not be overlooked.

In April and May 1941, Hurricanes were involved in the fall of Greece and Crete. They also flew in the Allied campaign in the Balkans. This began earlier in October 1940 when the Italian Army invaded Greece through Albania, only to be pushed back into Albania by the Greek Army, thus forcing Nazi Germany to intervene. Then, in April 1941, Axis forces involving German, Italian, Hungarian and Bulgarian military units, went into Greece and Yugoslavia. Yet the Battle of Greece – the attack on Greece by Italy and Germany in April 1941 – is sometimes less prominent in the story of the Second World War's Hurricanes.

The courage and skill of one truly outstanding Hurricane fighter pilot at this time was remarkable: that of a young South African called Marmaduke Thomas St John Pattle, DFC and Bar (1914–41). He was better known to the RAF as Pat Pattle.

## THE GREATEST HURRICANE ACE OF THE SECOND WORLD WAR?

Pat Pattle was a quiet, serious man with superb marksmanship and excellent eyesight. Born in the Cape Province in 1914, he was the son of English parents who had emigrated to South Africa.

At eighteen he joined the South African Airforce as a cadet. For some reason he was not accepted for air crew training. Yet the ambition to be a pilot was all too powerful and he travelled to England in 1936, where he joined the RAF aged twenty-two on a short service commission.

Pattle joined 80 Squadron in 1939. He was posted to Egypt on the outbreak of war. When hostilities began against Italy in June 1940, the squadron was moved to the Egyptian–Libyan border, and in his first months of combat operations against the Italian Regia Aeronautica, Pattle shot down two enemy fighters.

Despite flying an obsolete Gladiator in his early months of fighting, he soon gained a reputation as a superbly talented flyer, a man who could time his attacks to perfection.

On 2 December 1940, he shot down two observation planes, and two days later three Italian Falco CR42s were added to his tally during the Italian invasion of Egypt. Afterwards, his squadron was sent to Greece. On 20 February 1941, 80 Squadron was re-equipped with Hawker Hurricane Mark Is, replacing the Gladiators. On 28 February, 80 Squadron claimed the shooting down of twenty-seven Italian aircraft without loss in ninety minutes of air combat. Pattle personally claimed three kills in his Hurricane, shot down in less than three minutes. By mid-March 1941, he had been awarded the DFC. By then his tally was at least twenty-three enemy fighters destroyed. That same month, he was promoted to squadron leader.

On 6 April, when Hitler launched a massive invasion of Greece and Yugoslavia, all three Hurricane squadrons in the area were withdrawn to Eleusis, north of Athens. Pattle, now in command of 33 Squadron, was relentless. On 8 April, he shot down two Me 109s; the following day, he put paid to a German bomber. Yet as the Germans continued to destroy the Greek defences, Hurricane losses mounted.

By this time, Pattle was exhausted, feverish. He should have been stood down, but he insisted on continuing to fight. By dawn on Sunday 20 April, the Germans were well aware that British and Allied forces had begun preliminary withdrawal operations from ports in southern Greece, and that morning the Luftwaffe mounted mass attacks against Allied shipping in Piraeus harbour. Large formations appeared over Athens. Throughout a day of virtually continuous combat, Pattle led a formation of twelve Hurricanes over Athens. Five of the twelve Hurricanes were destroyed. Among them was Pattle himself, shot down and crashing into the sea around Athens, killed in the heat of battle at age twenty-seven.

Commemorated at the El Alamein Memorial, El Alamein, with the three thousand other Commonwealth airmen who lost their lives in the Middle Eastern theatre and have no known grave, he has been credited with shooting down at least forty aircraft, possibly fifty – which would make him the RAF's greatest Ace of the Second World War. But this remarkable achievement has never been formally recognized – for good reason.

During the mêlée of the 1941 Greek campaign and the German occupation of Greece, many documents, including Pat Pattle's diary and log book, were never recovered, due either to loss or destruction. Nonetheless, he remains an extraordinary hero.

## A VIVIDLY REMEMBERED SORTIE

During those chaotic days of April 1941, when 80 Squadron and their Hurricanes were fighting the enemy in the skies over Athens, another young RAF Hurricane airman from 80 Squadron – whose name would later become familiar across the world as a very famous author – was Roald Dahl.

Dahl (1916–90) flew as part of Pat Pattle's formation of twelve

Hurricanes during the Battle of Athens on 20 April. He had joined the RAF in 1939 and trained as a pilot officer in Iraq, later joining 80 Squadron when they had converted to Hurricanes.

Dahl vividly recalled his experiences during the Battle of Athens in several magazine articles and in his autobiography, *Going Solo*. In those hectic April weeks, he flew on sorties from Eleusis aerodrome three or four times a day, around twelve separate sorties in four days. Each sortie meant running across the airfield to where the Hurri was parked, starting up, taking off, flying to a nearby area, engaging with the enemy, getting home again, landing, reporting to the Ops Room, making sure the aircraft was refuelled and rearmed – in order to be ready for another take-off. He was well aware that the odds were not high for any RAF pilot taking off and returning alive.

Sometimes he flew above Piraeus harbour, chasing the Ju 88s bombing the shipping there. At other times he flew around the Lamia area, trying to deter the Luftwaffe from blasting away at the retreating army. Once or twice he met German bombers over Athens itself; usually they came along in groups of twelve at a time.

On three occasions, Dahl's Hurricane was badly shot up. Fortunately, the 80 Squadron riggers were skilled at patching up holes in the Hurricane's fuselage or mending a broken spar.

During those four intensely hectic days in April, individual victories were hardly noticed – everyone was frantically busy.

On 17 April, Dahl's log book recorded that two Hurricane pilots and both their aircraft were lost. The following day, another colleague went out and did not return. On 19 April, the squadron was left with twelve Hurricanes and twelve pilots. The day afterwards, Dahl went up four separate times. Most of all, he vividly remembered the first flight.

The authorities had decided that the entire force of

Hurricanes, all twelve of them, should go up together that day. It was thought that the sight of twelve RAF Hurricanes might boost the morale of the inhabitants. Around a hundred thousand German troops were advancing on the ground, and roughly a thousand German planes were within bombing distance.

On a beautiful spring morning at 10 a.m., all twelve Hurricanes took off one after the other over Eleusis airfield, heading for Athens, a few minutes' flying time away. Dahl had never flown a Hurricane in formation before. He'd done it once in training in a Tiger Moth. Round and round Athens they flew, Dahl trying to prevent his starboard wing-tip from scraping the plane next to him.

The formation was being led by Flight Lieutenant Pat Pattle, already a legend in the RAF, with many victories to his credit. Dahl had never spoken to him, but he had observed him in the mess tent several times, a small, soft-spoken man – who looked totally exhausted.

That morning, as Pat Pattle led his formation of twelve Hurricanes over Athens, they were flying at about 9,000 feet (2,743 m). Then, suddenly, the sky around them seemed to explode – German fighters, coming down from high above: Me 109s, also twin-engined 110s.

The Hurricane men broke formation. It was now every man for himself.

Dahl remembered seeing the tight little formation of Hurricanes peeling away, disappearing among the swarms of enemy fighters whizzing towards them from every side. They came from above and behind, and launched frontal attacks from ahead. He threw the Hurricane around as best he could, and whenever the enemy came into his sights, he pressed the button to aim his guns at the target.

He saw glimpses of planes with black smoke pouring from their engines, planes with pieces of metal flying off their fuselages. Bright red flashes came from the wings of the Messerschmitts as they fired their guns. One man whose Hurricane was in flames climbed calmly out onto a wing and jumped off.

Somehow Dahl managed to keep going until he had no ammunition left in his guns. He'd done a lot of shooting but he could not say whether he had shot anyone down or even hit any of them. He did not dare to pause for a fraction of a second to observe results. The sky was so full of aircraft that half the time was spent avoiding collisions. The German planes must surely have got in each other's way, because there were so many – yet so few Hurricanes.

Breaking away to dive for home, he knew his Hurricane had been hit, yet somehow he managed to steer the plane back and landed more or less safely at Eleusis. Taxiing to a parking place, he switched off the engine, slid back the hood. There he sat, taking deep gasping breaths, overwhelmed by the feeling he'd been in the fiery furnace and managed to claw his way out.

All around the sun was shining, wild flowers blossomed in the grass of the airfield.

Two airmen, a fitter and a rigger, came up to his Hurricane. They walked slowly all the way round it. The rigger, a middle-aged man, looked at him and said: 'Blimey mate, this kite's got so many 'oles in it, it looks like it's made of chicken-wire!'

Dahl knew they would do their best with it. He'd be needing it again very soon.

At the door of the little wooden operations room, three or four other pilots were standing around, each of them as soaking wet as he was, sweating as never before. His hand was shaking so much he couldn't light a cigarette. The other pilots' hands were shaking likewise. But he'd stayed up there for thirty minutes – and the enemy hadn't got him. Five out of the twelve Hurricane pilots in that battle hadn't been so lucky. One had bailed out and was saved. Four were killed.

Among the dead was Pat Pattle. The second most experienced pilot in the squadron, Flight Lieutenant Timber Woods, was also among those killed. Greek observers on the ground had seen five Hurricanes go down in smoke, but they also saw twenty-two Messerschmitts shot down during the battle, though no one in the squadron knew who got what.

Following the attack, 80 Squadron moved their base and later re-formed in Haifa, then Palestine. Dahl's RAF career continued; a period at the Air Ministry followed, then a posting as Assistant Air Attaché in Washington. By then his career was coupled with writing about his war experience: one vivid account had been published in the American publication, the *Saturday Evening Post*.

At the war's end, Roald Dahl opted to become a full-time writer. When he died in 1990, he had become one of the world's most famous authors, his books and films known worldwide, and musicals linked to his stories appearing frequently in London's West End theatres.

A most remarkable serviceman.

# CHAPTER 6

# THE FINAL YEARS

Variants of the Hurricane flew during the Second World War on twenty-three different battlefronts, making it the only Allied fighter to operate in every theatre of the Second World War.

As a fighter, the Hurricane was now outmoded. Faster, far more powerful and effective fighters had already been designed and tested since 1939.

Hurricane squadrons converted to Spitfires in some instances. The Hurricane was more or less phased out in northern Europe from 1942 onwards when the Hawker Typhoon, Hawker Tempest and de Havilland Mosquito became available in the following years.

Yet again, it was the skill and foresight of Sir Sydney Camm and his team at Hawker Aircraft that led to these improved, faster designs: the Hawker Typhoon and, later, the Hawker Tempest were already on the drawing board, even as the Hurricane Mark I was proving itself in 1940 during the Battle of Britain.

Camm had worked on the design concept of the Typhoon with the Air Ministry since 1939. A prototype was completed by January 1941. By late 1941, 150 Typhoons were with the RAF.

## HAWKER'S NEXT GENERATION

The Typhoon was originally intended as an interceptor to replace the Hurricane. Over time, however, it became established as a night-time intruder and long-range fighter.

By late 1942, it was equipped with bombs; towards the end of 1943, RP 3 (Rocket Projectile 3-inch [7.5-cm]) rockets were added, enabling it to become a successful ground-attack aircraft.

Twenty-six squadrons flew Hawker Typhoons during the June 1944 Normandy Landings (D-Day), successfully attacking German armoured divisions.

The Hawker Tempest was essentially a derivative of the Typhoon, originally known as Typhoon II. Many characteristics were identical to the Supermarine Spitfire. The Tempest was extremely fast at low altitudes – 457 mph (735 km/h) at 15,000 feet (4,572 m). Highly manoeuvrable and heavily armed, it emerged as one of the era's most successful low-level interceptor fighters, entering RAF service in 1944.

The Tempest proved especially effective against the threat of the German V-1 flying bomb (known as the doodlebug), targeting rail infrastructure as well as Luftwaffe aircraft on the ground. It was retired from service in 1953.


## 'IT WAS PART OF MY LIFE'

Squadron Leader Graham Leggett (see Chapter 5) was one pilot who took no great delight when his squadron, No. 73, made the conversion from Hurricanes to Spitfires in June 1943.

'There was jubilation from many pilots, though personally I was perfectly happy with the Hurricane. It was a plane I knew and could rely on. You could plop it down almost anywhere. Its rigidity had saved my neck more than once. I was quite excited about the transfer but I was not glad to see the back of the Hurricane.'

The Spitfire had many likeable attributes. But the switch, for him, was also the end of a relationship going back several years – when he had first joined Hawker Aircraft as an apprentice. The Hurricane, he admitted later, had become 'part of my life'.


## THE DIEPPE DISASTER

In August 1942, both the Hurricane and the Spitfire were involved in an exercise that was ill conceived and ultimately fatal for multitudes on the ground. The decision to attempt the Dieppe attack has long been a topic of controversy.

This was Operation Jubilee, an Allied amphibious attack on Dieppe on the north coast of German-occupied France. Dieppe was intensively fortified by the Germans. Yet the attack aimed to test German coastal defences in France – with the hope of seizing a French port.

It turned into tragedy. Over 6,000 infantry, nearly 5,000 of them Canadian, supported by a regiment of tanks, were put ashore, operating under the protection of RAF fighters.

The exercise was a fiasco.

Among the first to suffer casualties were eight squadrons of Hurricane dive-bombers converted to drop 250-lb (113-kg) or 500-lb (226-kg) bombs before an amphibious assault came in. The planes encountered intense German flak even as they approached the port. Twenty Hurricanes were shot down in the raid, twelve were damaged and fifteen pilots killed or captured. The RAF lost 106 aircraft: 88 were fighters, half of these were Spitfires. In less than twenty-four hours, more than half the infantry who had landed ashore had been killed, wounded or ended up as prisoners of war.

The Dieppe fiasco proved that the 250-lb or 500-lb bombs were not adequate for heavily fortified positions.

Why did the fiasco take place? Theories abound as to the rationale – one much-touted theory is that the raid was an attempt to steal the famous Enigma machine and code book from Dieppe. (Enigma was the encryption machine used by Germans to transmit coded messages.) Yet in simple terms, the tragic failure of Dieppe – especially disastrous for the Canadian forces – was due to extremely poor military planning, very shaky intelligence and Germany's own preparation for combat.

If 1942 was a tough time for Britain and its allies, one of the Second World War's most significant 'hinges of fate' occurred in a very different theatre of the Second World War during the last weeks of 1941.

## THE FAR EAST BURMA CAMPAIGN: DECEMBER 1941 – AUGUST 1945

This campaign encompassed a huge area of the globe: the Pacific Ocean and East and Southeast Asia. At the time, it was further away from home for the RAF than any other campaign it had been involved in.

Much of the fighting would take place in or over malaria-ridden jungles during drenching monsoon raids or on remote islands in searing tropical heat – with few navigational aids available.

In this environment, soldiers and airmen from British Commonwealth troops and their Allies effectively became 'one force' in a war waged against Japan, a tenacious, often brutal foe prepared to fight at any cost.

This globalization of the Second World War started on 7 December 1941 when a Japanese task force attacked the US naval base at Pearl Harbor and America entered the conflict. The Pearl Harbor attack came as a surprise, though Japan and the US had been edging towards conflict for many decades.

At the start of America's entry into the Second World War, aircraft numbers located in the region were pitifully small for such a vast area. In December 1941, there were just 265 front-line aircraft to cover Malaya, Borneo and Hong Kong. These were mostly the Brewster Buffalo – American monoplane fighters – with just four recently formed squadrons, many of which were flown by young Australian and New Zealand pilots.

Moreover, there was little awareness of the opposition the RAF and the Allies were about to face.

## THE FALL OF SINGAPORE

Just one day after Pearl Harbor came another totally unexpected shock. On 8 December 1941, Singapore, then an outpost of the British Empire – and the foremost British military base and economic port in Southeast Asia – was subjected to heavy bombing by long-range Japanese aircraft. Other British outposts, including Hong Kong, were also attacked by Japanese aircraft. Japanese troops landed in British-held Malaya and Borneo, as well as several Allied-held staging posts in the Pacific Ocean, while others headed towards Singapore.

In the first months of 1942, the Japanese launched further attacks against Burma (now known as Myanmar, then a British colony), Australian-administered New Guinea and Papua, and the islands of the then Dutch East Indies (now known as Indonesia).

The Japanese made rapid advances through the jungle and captured Singapore on 15 February 1942. For British Prime Minister Winston Churchill, news of the fall of Singapore was devastating. He described it as 'the worst disaster' and 'largest capitulation' in British military history.

By that time, the air defenders of Singapore consisted of biplane bombers and the Brewster Buffalo – as well as ten Hurricane fighters of 232 Squadron, based at Kellang airfield. More Hurricanes – fifty-one Mark IIs – were sent to join them in December 1941 with five RAF squadrons. They arrived in Singapore late in January 1942.

By then, the RAF's fighter force was completely outnumbered and frequently outmatched by the Japanese fighters, specifically the Mitsubishi Zero, a single-seat low-wing monoplane.

The Japanese Zero carried no armour for the pilot. Nor did it carry a bullet-proof windscreen or self-sealing fuel tanks. Fast and agile, these planes were not easily shot down. They were more manoeuvrable than any Allied aircraft flying at that time. They were there to attack and kill – or be killed. Only in 1943 would the tide turn against them when more capable Allied fighters were introduced.

By the time the fifty-one Hurricanes arrived, the Buffalos had been overwhelmed. The existing Hurricanes, in turn, had suffered heavy losses in dogfights. The Hurricane could fight the Zero at altitudes above 20,000 feet (6,096 m), but at the lower level, where most combat occurred, the Japanese planes were taking a very heavy toll.

Terence Kelly (1920–2013) joined 3 Squadron in May 1941, aged twenty. He'd had 220 hours' flying time on Hurricane Mark II s when his next Squadron, 258 Hurricane Squadron, based at Kenley, Kent, was posted to the Middle East. By then he'd experienced a dozen 'rhubarbs' (RAF patrols over enemy-occupied territory made by single fighters under cloud cover).

Kelly was shocked by what he found when he arrived with his squadron in Singapore.

'When we landed on 29 January 1942 at Selatar aerodrome on Singapore Island, within ten minutes of ordering a drink in the mess, we realized that the pall of defeatism was so thick, you could have cut it with a knife.'

The following day, he and Pilot Officer Bruce McAlister from the Royal New Zealand Air Force were taking their Hurricanes out of their packing cases, wanting to get them clean and ready to fight, helped by British ground staff. At that point, a Japanese aircraft started circling, very high, over the airfield. The ground staff, already extremely nervous, began making for the jungle, seeking cover. They'd already had more than enough of the terrifying Japanese onslaught.

The two newly arrived airmen had no option but to point their revolvers at the ground staff and say: 'Stay there until we say you can go.'

In the event, neither 258 Squadron nor Kelly could do very much flying in Singapore since there were so few serviceable aircraft: just eight Hurricanes. When they did take off on 30 January, one Japanese bomber was shot down.

Pilot Officer Bruce Alexander McAlister, twenty-four, from Invercargill, New Zealand, was killed that day in combat with two Japanese Zeros. McAlister had joined the New Zealand RAF in 1940 and had flown with 258 Squadron in defensive patrols in Malta until the news came through of the Japanese raid on Pearl Harbor, upon which the squadron was sent off to Singapore. He too had been based at RAF Kenley.

His body was never found. He is commemorated in Singapore at the Singapore Memorial and at his family memorial in Invercargill's Eastern Cemetery.

On 30 January, forty-eight Hurricane IIAs arrived on the aircraft carrier HMS *Indomitable*. They flew to airfields near the island of Sumatra in Indonesia. Japanese air raids destroyed a large number of Hurricanes on the ground in both Singapore and Sumatra.

On 8 February, a series of dogfights over Singapore took place. Ten Hurricanes scrambled to intercept eighty Japanese aircraft. The Hurricanes shot down six Japanese planes, with one loss. The air battles continued.

By then it was obvious that with so few RAF aircraft remaining, the surviving Hurricanes, including the one flown by Terence Kelly, had to withdraw to the island of Sumatra.

The Japanese now had control of the sky.

No. 258 Squadron remained in Sumatra, facing close to annihilation. Out of twenty-two pilots of the squadron listed in October 1941 – comprising British, New Zealand, American, Canadian, Rhodesian and Australian pilots – six were killed in action, three were killed in flying accidents, one died after the war from wounds, and five became Japanese prisoners of war.

Terence Kelly continued to fly cannon-firing Hurricane

IICs in Sumatra during the brave attempt by the Hurricane squadrons to stop the Japanese invaders. But by mid-February, Sumatra was overrun and the surviving Hurricanes retreated to Java, another island in Indonesia, joined by reinforcements flown in from HMS *Indomitable*.

The brutal Japanese onslaught continued. Terence Kelly fought valiantly in a series of bitterly contested aerial engagements in Java against the Japanese Zeros. By March 1942, there were just four remaining Hurricanes and pilots from 258 Squadron and a group of New Zealanders who had a few Hurricanes. They continued to fly the Hurricanes until they were exhorted to get away, escape somehow. Only they could not. They were captured by the Japanese. Of the twenty-two pilots of 258 Squadron, just seven survived – including Terence Kelly, taken prisoner by the Japanese.

Kelly spent nearly three years in a Japanese prison camp located in Innoshima Island, just a few miles away from the first-ever deployed atomic bomb explosion over Hiroshima in August 1945. Most of the 5,100 RAF men who became prisoners of war in the Pacific/Far East campaign fell, like Kelly, into Japanese hands. Of these, 1,700 died in captivity.

Released in 1945 when the Second World War ended, Kelly returned to the UK and worked as a businessman. He also wrote a series of books about his wartime experiences, including a powerful memoir, *By Hellship to Hiroshima*. The memoir, translated into Japanese, recounts the horrific story of his transport, by ship, to Innoshima Island, where he was forced to repair crane trucks while evading the bombs that were continuously dropped on the island in the last months of the Second World War.

Burma (Myanmar) soon followed Java in the continued Japanese invasion of the region. The Japanese launched their aerial attack on Myanmar's capital, Rangoon, on 23 January, aimed at neutralizing the small RAF force based in and around Rangoon. By then, more Hurricane fighters had been moved from the Middle East.

Three squadrons, 17, 135 and 136, were moved to nearby India with detachments operating from Mingaladon airfield near Rangoon. A squadron of Bristol Blenheims and thirty Hurricane fighters also arrived in Rangoon to provide some offensive capability, joining the American Volunteer Group (the Flying Tigers) and the Indian air force equipped with Westland Lysanders.

The defences of Burma, however, could not possibly prevail against the invading Japanese. In early March 1942, the capital, Rangoon, and its vital port were defeated. The RAF and the incoming Hurris had done their best in the struggle to defend the city, but as the Japanese continued to push north, the surviving British and Commonwealth troops had no choice but to retreat to India across nearly a thousand miles (1,609 km) of difficult terrain.

The next three years in this global war saw the Americans and the British focusing on 'Germany first'; the idea for what was now taking place in the Pacific Ocean and Southeast Asia was to hold the line and build up the Indian bases necessary to recover Burma. The US prepared to use India as a base, amassing strong forces in north-east India in 1943–4 while the RAF played a major part in the air supply operations in Burma.

Joint RAF and naval operations made a difference: aircraft were invaluable for rescue operations – often over great distances.

Burma was among the toughest of all territories: almost cut off by mountain ranges to the east, north and west, the land route was hilly, often impassable, so the joint Allied Armies depended on air power far more than they had in any other Second World War campaign.

Seasonal weather, dry in the early months of the year but with drenching monsoons arriving in May until the autumn, made for the very worst conditions for flying and ground fighting.

## FLYING THE BOAT BUSTERS IN INDIA

Jim Ashworth from British Columbia, Canada (born in 1919), served with the Royal Canadian Air Force and military for twenty-six years. He won a Burma Star for his services in RAF 20 Squadron during the Second World War, a campaign medal awarded to British and Commonwealth forces who saw active service in the Second World War's Burma campaign.

Jim completed training in Alberta in 1941 and arrived in England later that year, joining the RAF at Staverton, Gloucestershire. The RAF wanted Jim to become an instructor, but he was determined to be a fighter pilot. Eventually he, along with other young Canadians, was sent to the RAF Advanced Flying Unit for pilots in Peterborough, Cambridgeshire. Training started on Miles Masters, then upgraded to Hurricanes.

Jim graduated from the OTU (an RAF Operational Training Unit) in Scotland in July 1942. In October 1942, following a lengthy maritime voyage, he arrived in Purulia, a road and rail junction in West Bengal. He was assigned to fly with RAF 20 Squadron, an army cooperative squadron, supporting the 14th Army already engaged in the vicious jungle war against the Japanese. (The 14th is sometimes regarded as the 'Forgotten Army', consisting of troops from all corners of the then British Commonwealth: by 1945 it was the world's largest army, at around one million men.)

Jim was now flying the Hurricane IID, equipped with a 40-mm (1.6-in) Bofors gun, an anti-aircraft cannon. He was stationed on the south coast of India at a station called Chiringa, close to the border with Burma, then occupied by the Japanese.

> 'We could take off and land right on the beach. They laid down chain link fence on the sand to stabilize it. It worked very well.'

The IIDs were known as tank busters. But in Burma they became known as 'boat busters'.

Jim's action relied on the Army Liaison Officer, who would provide the targets shown as coordination pinpoints on maps. Many were unseen targets in thick jungle. Others were tanks, gun emplacements, vehicles and steamers.

A Calcutta newspaper clipping dated 1943 is headed: HURRICANES GO BOAT BUSTING.

> Hurricanes armed with 40-mm cannon are playing havoc with Jap river supply lines in the Maungdaw, Buthidaung, Akyab and Minyba areas. In the past month they have flown more than 100 sorties from an advanced airfield in East Bengal and this is their bag:
>
> 1 large river steamer, 60 feet [18 m] long
>
> 75 large sampans [A sampan is a small boat, frequently used in East Asia]
>
> 119 small sampans
>
> 47 *kisties* – shallow draught country boats
>
> 46 dugouts – enclosed canoes, 20–25 feet [6–7.5 m] long.

Originally fitted in the Middle East for tank busting, 40-mm cannon are ideal against river-craft. Two of their armour-piercing rounds will knock the bottom clean out of most small boats.

## MAZE OF WATERWAYS

The whole of the area between Maungdaw and Akyab is one vast maze of waterways. Its few roads are little more than tracks and totally unsuited for road transport. Japanese troops were largely dependent on rivers for supplies, and a daily shuttle patrol of two Hurricane boat busters made their job as tough as possible.

In addition, the squadron was often called to give close support to advance units of the 14th Army and cooperate with Vengeance dive-bombers against Japanese bunkers.

Recalled Jim:

'The Japanese were using the Kaladan River to freight their supplies and equipment. Our mission was to fly low down the river. If we saw any ships we would fire on them. We were careful not to hit any sampans being used by the Burmese who were friendly to us. To try to bring us down, the Japanese strung steel cables across the Kaladan River at various points, which were a major concern. We also watched the roads and fired on tanks, transport vehicles, anything that looked military.'

He recalled major successes on a large river steamer near Akyab and an important fuel-supply depot east of the village.

'We had two 40-millimetre cannons mounted underneath the aircraft with high-explosive shells, so powerful that when we fired them the recoil would slow us down 15 knots.'

Armour plates had been added to the radiator, motor and underneath the seat. But the added weight made the Hurricane more difficult to manoeuvre. Several pilots were killed when trying to pull up in mountainous terrain.

'They didn't have much room. Most of the missions were flown at less than 5,000 feet [1,524 m], sometimes as low as 1,000 feet [305 m]. Or lower. When you spotted something you wanted to take out you had to get right down there.'

Being stationed close to the front helped in one way.

'We didn't have far to fly. The Hurricane had enough fuel for about two hours and thirty minutes, so all my missions were shorter than that though I cut it pretty close sometimes.'

The pilots flew in pairs. On one occasion they were returning from a mission in south-west India when their radio communication failed with their home base.

'We were above the clouds over the western Ghats [a mountain range] looking for an opening. You couldn't just drop down to take a look – you might fly straight into a mountain. Finally, we dropped below 800 feet [244 m] looking for a clue as to where we were. Nothing.

'We eventually ran so low on fuel we had to come down in a rice paddy. That was a close call.

'I hired a couple of Indians to guard the aircraft and we walked into the nearby village and sent a telegram to home base and they sent out somebody with extra fuel.'

Living conditions were poor and food rations short. The weather, too, was always a factor.

'We couldn't fly at all during monsoon season and there were some very serious thunderstorms.'

During the siege of Imphal from March to July 1944 in north-east India, the squadron was also called upon to deliver food.

'The Japanese had tried to invade India but were driven back into Burma with heavy losses. For weeks the Allied forces at Imphal were surrounded and cut off.'

The Battle of Imphal is still considered to be a turning point on the Southeast Asian front. Everything had to be flown in.

'My squadron based at Chittagong provided four aircraft, rotating three or four weeks depending on weather. We packed as much food as we could carry into our small aircraft and landed inside enemy territory.'

The squadron was also required to drop leaflets behind enemy lines, rallying the Burmese people to resist the enemy. The Japanese were doing the same thing inside India. Mostly, however, it was trying to cripple the enemy, often in very dangerous circumstances.

'The Japanese were doing their best to shoot us down with their anti-aircraft guns and they often succeeded. One week we lost seven guys.'

Jim's best week was in June 1944 at Imphal.

'I remember looking down the barrel of a big 105-millimetre [4-in] anti-aircraft gun while I was strafing their gun placements along the Tiddim Road. That was pretty frightening. But I was successful against a cruiser tank and several tankettes in the area. It was an important mission to open the Tiddim Road and we did it.'

(The Tiddim Road battles were some of the fiercest in the entire Burma war, with a profound influence on its outcome.)

Soon afterwards, Jim went down with malaria and was in hospital. While he was there, a friend went out to the Tiddim Road, located the Japanese tank that Jim had destroyed, and brought back the identification plate for him.

Jim's RAF 20 Squadron crest had the Japanese tank plate screwed onto the right corner. The 20 Squadron crest depicts a rising sun with an eagle perched on a curved sabre, indicative of the squadron's work with the army in India. The squadron's motto is: *Facta non Verba*: Deeds not Words.

Not long after he was pronounced free of malaria, Jim succumbed to dengue fever, another infectious tropical disease. It marked the end of Jim's wartime history in Burma. After eighteen months in India and more than fifty missions, he returned to England and then to Canada. His career with the Royal Canadian Air Force continued until his retirement in 1966. Then Jim and his wife and daughter moved to Invermere, British Columbia, in the heart of the Canadian Rockies.

In May 2020, inspired by another Burma veteran, Captain Sir Thomas Moore (1920–2021) – known throughout the world as 'Captain Tom' – walked 100 laps of his back garden for charity in his hundredth year and raised £33 million (over $41 million) for the NHS. Jim Ashworth, then aged 101, walked four blocks each day to raise over $100,000 (£830,000) for a local food bank in 2020.

Deeds not words. Yet again.

## A TERRIFYING TREK THROUGH THE JUNGLE

Another Canadian Hurricane pilot, Squadron Leader Bob Johnson, who died aged ninety-six in 2015, told an equally remarkable story of his time in Burma in 1945 after being shot down.

He was with 28 Squadron, flying IIDs on reconnaissance missions. The squadron was based at Kalemyo in the Kabaw Valley, Burma.

On the early morning of 14 January, Bob was briefed to do a reconnaissance of roads, bridges and waterways in the Pokakku-Pagan area along the Irrawaddy River. The object was to determine the Japanese lines of communication over which troops and supplies were being transported. His no. 2 was Flight Lieutenant Gavin Douglas, an experienced pilot but on his first operational mission.

'We got airborne around 8 a.m. and travelled to the target area at low level. It was a nice sunny day and the flight was uneventful as we skimmed over trees and paddy fields. I did a close inspection at low-level roads and bridges and then headed south along the Irrawaddy.

'No Japanese were seen and only a few bullock carts were moving along the roads. As we went south, Douglas was about 25 feet [7.5 m] off the water and line abreast on my port side.

'A short distance south of Pagan at a point where a small *chaung* [a mountain stream] came in from the east I saw some movement. I swung left, crossing close behind Douglas to check it out. I then saw a large river boat a short distance up the *chaung* and a dozen or more men loading large petrol or oil drums.

'It was only seconds since I first swung left and I was now in a steep turn around the mast of the boat when there were two heavy impacts on my aircraft.

'I knew at once I'd been hit with fairly heavy flak. I headed north-west across the river gaining some height and told Douglas over the radio that I'd been hit. There was a hole at the bottom of my aircraft between my feet, and glycol was spraying up. The other strike must have been on the engine.

'A quick check of the instrument panel indicated I was about 1,588 feet [484 m], engine temperature was rising and oil pressure was almost zero. Smoke was coming from the engine. I was now west of the Irrawaddy and approaching the Yaw Chaung [a tributary of the Irrawaddy].

'It looked too rough for a forced landing so I decided to bail out. I told Douglas by radio of my intention and I heard him say 'good luck old chap'. I was losing height but I stayed with it until I was passing over a village on the west bank of the Yaw Chaung. At that point

I was very low, so jettisoned the canopy and tried to climb out. I had difficulty standing up so jettisoned the escape panel on the starboard side and rolled out. I saw the tail plane pass in front of my face then pulled the ripcord.

'I landed with a jar and tumbled sideways. I was on top of a ridge with a deep gully to the north. My pistol was missing, probably caught on the aircraft as I rolled out. I snapped off my escape kit from under the parachute seat cushion and ran to the west along the ridge.

'Within a few minutes I heard voices so I went into the gully. The wireless cord was a bother so I yanked the earphones from my helmet and stuffed masks, cord and phones into a hole in the ground. I ran west along the gully. About five minutes later I heard a lot of yelling, then saw people about 50 yards [46 m] away running toward me along the ridge on the north side of the gully. There were others on the south ridge ahead of me.

'I climbed the north ridge and slid down a steep slope, the only cover was low scrub bush. By chance I slid into a shallow depression in the hillside 18 inches [46 cm] or so deep and the bush was more dense here. I burrowed in, pulling the foliage over me and remained motionless. The voices were suddenly loud and very close.

'I carefully slid my knife out but did not move. People came so close I thought they would hear my heart pounding but I was not discovered. At one point I looked up the hill and saw a Japanese soldier with a rifle on top of the ridge. The talking and shouting would sometimes be very close to me and sometimes at a distance; there was also the barking of dogs. I decided to stay under cover until dark and during the long wait I debated with myself the pros and cons of surrendering or fighting should I be discovered.

'I decided that if there was only one soldier I would try to silence him quickly but otherwise I'd surrender and hope for the best. It was an immense relief when darkness came and all was quiet.

'I waited another hour or so before leaving my hiding place then climbed to the ridge and followed it west. I moved very cautiously, stopping to listen at frequent intervals, and then the ridge levelled out. I continued west until I was getting close to a village.

'I gave the village a wide berth and was then in rough undulating terrain with thin bush. Walking was difficult and tiring. With the first glimmer of light in the sky I found a hiding place among roots of an old dead tree. It had been washed out and was almost like a cave. After prodding around for snakes I crawled in.

'I dozed off and on and, as the day progressed I occasionally heard aircraft in the near distance, which sounded like Hurricanes. Probably search aircraft from 28 Squadron. Having managed to avoid capture and to even get a short distance away was a great boost to my morale. All was quiet; I judged I must be at least a few miles beyond the village I had passed.

'I had been using my escape kit as a pillow. How fortunate I was to have such a well-stocked kit – I had sewn it together by hand.

'Regulation escape gear was a coverall-type garment with a lot of pockets for maps, etc. I'd found the garment much too hot to wear when flying low level behind a heat-producing Rolls-Royce Merlin and the pockets were not too adequate anyway.

'A lot of our missions were a long way behind enemy lines. I had concluded that if one were to survive in a hostile environment it would be necessary to be self-sufficient for a reasonable period of time.

'I cut up some khaki trousers and fashioned a square bag the size of a parachute cushion with a slit in the centre for the harness. I sewed it by hand with buttons on a flap on the top. Two straps also made of cloth were sewn on. I extended the tabs, which normally held the sponge cushion on top of the parachute, so the kit, which when filled was 3 to 4 inches [7.5 to 10 cm] thick, would be under the cushion.

'Now it was time to take stock of supplies and decide on a plan of action. I had three metal tins containing Horlicks tablets [malted milk wafers], Benzedrine tablets, chewing gum, fish line and hooks, salt tablets, needle and thread, mepacrine tablets [essential in the Far East at the time to prevent malaria], water-sterilizing crystals and some bandage and sulpha powder. I also had a bar of hard chocolate, a canvas water *chargal* [a type of water carrier] a flashlight with good batteries, a money belt [for Indian rupees] a magnifying glass, a metal mirror and maps and compasses. The best compass was a regulation marching compass with luminous dial with V sight and mirrored top for taking back bearings. My wrist watch was also luminous. The maps I had for the mission covered the area over which I would need to travel but I had others if I wandered too far astray.

'As a reconnaissance pilot I was familiar with map

reading so with a good compass and maps I was confident of being able to steer a course.

'I was wearing heavy leather boots, thick wool socks, tropical-weight green battle dress and a flying helmet now without earphones. I had a clean white handkerchief and a regulation knife with a 7-inch-thick [18-cm] blade.

'I studied the maps and decided on a course. The map indicated there was a track more or less following the *chaung* and I would then be heading almost due north and could follow the mountains until I got into the Gangaw valley. Our forces had been advancing in this direction when I left. I estimated it might take me twenty-four to thirty days to reach Gangaw.

'I counted the Horlicks and on a ration of six a day there were enough to last thirty-eight days. I would nibble sparingly of the chocolate until it was gone. The immediate problem was water and I was already very thirsty. The map indicated I would be in barren rough country to begin with but there were some small *chaungs* marked where I should be able to find water.

'I would avoid contact with Burmese if at all possible. It would be safer to travel by night and hide during the day and I'd conserve energy when it was cool. Night travel would be slower but I concluded safety and conservation of energy were more important. I repacked my kit with the flashlight on top and put one tin containing Horlicks in a breast pocket and a map in another pocket. I had a piece of string tied to the marching compass which would be tied to my web belt.

'I felt very good about having made these plans and

was anxious for nightfall to get moving. Two Horlicks for breakfast, two for lunch and two just before dark did not do much to satisfy hunger and it was not easy to swallow a mepacrine tablet without water. I tried chewing some grass hoping for some moisture but the taste was dreadful and my mouth and tongue felt dryer than before. I studied the map, committing to memory the general rise and fall of the ground and any salient points I might be able to pick out at night.

'I waited until it was truly dark. The sky was clear and having noted a compass course I used a bright star in the western sky as guide. The constellation of Orion was due east and readily distinguishable so I used it constantly. There was only scrub bush in the rough hilly country, no sign of habitation. The first stream bed I came upon was dry. With my knife and hands I dug 2 to 3 feet [61–90 cm] but no sign of moisture.

'On two other occasions that night I came upon dried-up streambeds and though I dug a number of holes there was no moisture. By the time the sky started to lighten I was feeling very tired and discouraged at not finding water. I convinced myself I'd be more fortunate the next night. I found a fairly dense clump of bush that would provide both concealment and shade.

'The night had been quite cool but the day was hot and again I had difficulty swallowing the mepacrine and Horlicks. I dozed off and on and resisted the urge to move by daylight. Again I studied the map and when darkness came, set off using the stars as guides.

'My efforts at finding water were a repeat of the previous night. By the time the sky brightened I was very tired, in low spirits. Again I found a place to hide and keep out of the sun. By then I realized how essential it was to avoid the sun, rest as much as I could.

'I had not found the two tracks that were there according to the map and concluded there was a chance the map was inaccurate or the tracks were no longer used and had drifted over. There was no way of being certain I was on my intended course.

'I was discouraged and at times visualized simply perishing: I'd never be found and the vultures would make short work of me. I often thought of my family in Canada and wondered if they knew what had happened. At times I dreamed of guzzling quarts of ice cold milk, eating all sorts of nice food.

'It was now the fourth day. Digging for water took a lot of time, and by this time, my fingers were raw and sore. I was afraid of infection. I decided not to dig for water and I would then be able to cover more ground.

'I set off again after dark and had walked only an hour or so when I had to stop for a rest. I do not remember starting up again but suddenly found myself stumbling along and came to the terrifying realization the kit was not on my back.

'In a state of panic, I searched for it. I started a systematic search trying to retrace my steps in a series of square search patterns. About three hours later I found some of my tracks in the sand and there was the kit in the place I had stopped to rest. I was so exhausted I fell asleep and did not awaken until daylight.

'I don't remember much of the next 3 days and nights. My tongue was swollen, my throat parched and I seemed to have a continuous high temperature. After midnight on the seventh night I came upon a bullock cart track which ran north.

'I followed it north and realized I was walking in soft mud. I soon found myself in water a few inches deep. I gulped and gulped until I regurgitated. I'd been gulping half mud, half water. The water was probably used as a watering place for water buffalo; looking for the deepest part I drank some clearer water.

'After soaking the water *chargal* [a desert water vessel] I filled it with reasonably clear water and tied it to my web belt with the cloth straps from the *chargal*. I felt a village would not be far off and there'd probably be a source of water, such as a stream. I continued north, found the village and since all was quiet circled it at a short distance but did not find any water.

'I followed the track north and when daylight was near, found a hiding place a quarter-mile [0.4 km] or so west of the cart track. The vegetation was reasonably dense so it was not difficult to find a safe place.

'Though I heard voices in the distance I slept more than usual during the day, confident I'd now be able to find a stream and resolved not to stray very far from water at any time. I sipped sparingly of the murky water I'd doctored with sterilizing crystals: about half remained at day's end.

'Again, I waited until the sun was well below the mountains in the west, then headed north looking for the Yaw C [a river]. I lost the cart track and found myself in quite dense bush. Progress was slow so at daylight when all was quiet I decided to continue walking for an hour or so. Then I suddenly found I was close to the edge of what appeared to be a clearing.

'Moving cautiously forward I saw a native woman with a basket on her head walking along a path toward me. I dropped to my knees. She came slowly toward me, peering into the bush with a wide grin on her face; it was obvious she was aware of something. I tried to pretend I was a dog, making barking noises, but she was not fooled. She parted the bushes, I stood up and stepped forward.

'Her expression changed. I pointed to her basket and by signs indicated I wanted something to eat. She shook her head and hurried off in a northerly direction along a cart track.

'I crossed the track and open area and crouched in the bush. I could see the woman was going directly to some huts. A number of native men brandishing bamboo staves and shouting ran out from among the huts. I ran away from the track, making a lot of noise in my haste.

'The shouting got louder so I scrambled into a very dense clump of bush, pulled twigs and leaves over myself, then remained still. The shouting came closer, then started to fade. I realized the natives were following the track, thinking I had gone in that direction. I moved off to the west, stopping frequently to listen, and after a few miles found a good hiding place.

'Although I was almost exhausted when I stopped I was so apprehensive of having been followed I slept very little during the day and vowed I'd stick to night travel only.

'I could not come to a conclusion as to my position. I finished off the little water remaining in the *chargal*: I'd have to find more soon. It was obvious I was still south of the Yaw C but since it swung north in a big loop I might still be more than a night's travel from it.

'My spirits alternately soared and sagged. I was tempted to try the Benzedrine but since I'd been told that the high it produced was followed by a low I resisted.

'The next night was uneventful other than walking in dense growth over hilly terrain. I did not find any water. Insects were now more plentiful but since it was the dry season fortunately there were no leeches.

'During the day I saw innumerable large webs with great hairy spiders waiting for their prey. I did not know if any were poisonous but they were so obnoxious I avoided them like the plague.

'The following night I was still not sure of my position and due to denser growth the stars were not always in view. It was impossible to hold a steady course.

'I resorted to using the compass more often and occasionally when it felt safe I would shield the flashlight with my handkerchief so only a glimmer of light was visible and try to relate particularly high rises of ground to map contours. It was obvious I covered a lot of ground without advancing a great distance.

'My strength was holding up. After midnight I came across another cart track and following it to the north I found another water hole, larger and deeper than the first one. Putting my handkerchief over my face I sucked water through it and felt quite refreshed.

'I looked for a village, which was no doubt far away. The ground was now sloping away sharply in front and I suddenly heard a dog bark. On creeping forward I saw a lot of *bashas* and could smell smoke along with the aroma of food. [A *basha* is a waterproof canvas or plastic sheet with eyelets or loops in the perimeter used in outdoor or military situations to act as a shelter.] Thinking I might be able to find a cooking pot with dregs in it I started entering the village.

'Other dogs were barking but they did not follow when I made a hasty retreat. I heard voices; some villagers were awakened. I decided trying to steal food wasn't worth the risk as long as I had Horlicks. The sloping of the ground indicated the village may have been near a stream so I moved away to the west for a distance, then followed the slope to the north.

'It was not yet daybreak and I began to hear voices and other sounds not too far away, so I decided I'd find a hiding place for the day. Returning to the densely covered hills I entered a small clearing on the side of the hill when I heard an animal bark.

'I heard the same sound several times during the night; it didn't sound like a dog's bark. I was motionless when suddenly a small deer burst from the bush into the clearing, wheeled away and gave another loud bark as it crashed into the bush. I saw a short white tail and heard other deer jump into motion, crash off through the bush.

'It was a relief to know the bark was not from some ferocious animal. It was quite cool so I thought I'd rest at the edge of the bush until the sun came out. I drifted off to sleep. I was suddenly aware of something but didn't know what. I had become accustomed to awakening yet remaining motionless until I was aware of my surroundings and I heard nothing, but felt a slight movement on my legs.

'Still without moving I glanced down and saw a snake

about three feet [90 cm] long slithering across my legs below the knees. It continued moving and disappeared in twigs and leaves along the side of the hill. I thought it was a cobra.

'It was the only snake I saw on my trek though there were undoubtedly plenty around. This was why I'd chosen to wear heavy boots and gaiters [a protective fabric guard] as part of my flying gear.

'I had water in my *chargal* and felt I was getting close to the Yaw C. I set off on a westerly course that night and sure enough it wasn't long before I found the elusive stream, a milestone, as I'd now be in country where map reading would be easier and water no longer a problem. I heard a gurgling sound in the near distance and soon found the junction where the Kin Chang [a waterfall] came in from the south.

'I stripped off, wallowed in the cool water, rinsed my *chargal* and refilled it. With my boots and clothes in a bundle, which I held over my head I forded the Kin C. After dressing I set off along the gravelled bank on the south side of the Yaw C. The stream did not follow a straight course; it was so much better than walking through the forest.

'Before daybreak I heard the sound of natives and water buffalo ahead. I stopped at once and a voice called out. There was some conversation and the voices came closer so I scrambled up the bank into some thorn bushes and remained quiet. The natives did not climb the bank, I heard them going to and fro. After a time all was quiet so I moved off into the hills and found a hiding place for the day.

'I was elated at having found the junction of two

streams. There should now be no problem following the Yaw C as it wound its way down narrow valleys, the track more or less parallel to it. When the Yaw swung off to the west, just north of the village of Pasok, there was a track that led through the mountains to Gangaw.

'I was now in very hilly country, the beginning of the Chin mountains [north-west Burma] covered mostly with bamboo forest. Walking was not too difficult so I could move more or less parallel to the stream until I was beyond the village.

'At one point I went into a depression between two hills and suddenly the bamboos were alive with monkeys everywhere, shrieking and howling, obviously very agitated.

'I had seen monkeys attack and claw a friend when he teased them with a banana. I retreated up the slope and was thankful they did not follow further than the crest of the hill. It meant a lot of walking but I gave the narrow valley a wide berth and eventually went to the stream to wash up and fill the *chargal*. The rest of the night was uneventful and at daybreak I took refuge in the high hills away from the stream.

'That night I was still heading west when I came upon a car track, and the junction of a small *chaung*. Thinking I was in the vicinity of a village where the Yaw swung north I crossed the Yaw, followed a track heading north. It soon petered out so I did a zigzag course trying to find the Yaw again.

'By daylight I had not found it. I was lost. I finally climbed a high peak to find a landmark. From this I saw that the hills sloped away to the east and almost at the horizon I saw the sun shining on a broad river curving down from the north at a point where a smaller river joined it from the west.

'I recognized it as the junction of the Kyaw River and Yaw Chaung. Looking west where the mountains rose sharply I saw a prominent peak marked on the quarter-inch [0.6-cm] map near the village of Kanpetlet about 20 miles [32 km] to the south-west.

'I took a back bearing with my compass and an approximate fix on my position. I was about 4 miles [6.5 km] north of where I should be. I decided to rest during the day and retrace my path to the Yaw C at night.

'As the sun was sinking I headed south and in time came to the Yaw C and picked up my intended course. By daybreak I was near the village of Kyaukleit and found a thick bush in which to hide for the day. During the day women and children came to visit the place only about 150 feet [46 m] from where I was hiding. I could hear voices and sounds from the village through the day and was not able to sleep much.

'When darkness came and the villagers seemed to have bedded down I moved off to the west looking for a village where the Yaw came down from the north. I forded a stream and when I could not find the cart track I was looking for, crossed the stream and found the village, which I circled before returning to the stream again.

'On approaching the water I was aware there were about half a dozen people stretched out sleeping and a number of rafts on which there were large wicker baskets. I was about two feet [60 cm] from one man. He was covered with a blanket and his head was on a pack.

'I was certain he was Japanese. Moving with extreme caution, keeping a watch on the sleeping men, I walked backwards until I was off the gravel.

'I found the track I'd been looking for and followed it north. I skirted one more village and by daybreak had reached the village of Pasok. I found a place to hide in the hills overlooking the large village and fell asleep.

'The sun was well above the horizon when I was awakened by the sound of singing and chanting. I covered myself with twigs and remained quiet. The singing came very close on the hillside below me and I saw a group of about twenty native men.

'They had long wide-bladed knives with large handles with which they were chopping down bamboo trees. The path they had followed up the hill was below me and they were working their way down the hill. This continued until afternoon so again I did not get too much rest.

'When darkness came I found the cart track and followed it to the north. I had travelled a few miles when I heard bullock carts coming down the track towards me. I hid in the bushes until they passed, then carried on walking. I had not gone far when I came upon a cart stopped on the track. I could not pass it readily without being seen.

'Natives did not generally move about at night but I knew the Japanese did. I decided to detour.

'I went across country back to the Yaw C and followed the stream until it was time to take cover for the day. There was no sound to suggest there was any habitation near so I washed my socks and spread my clothes to dry while basking in the sun.

'I dozed during the day. It was a week or so and I was now at higher altitude and nights were quite cool. This was noticeable when I was wet from wading across streams. There had been no rain. I hadn't found any berries or other edible growth.

'The Horlicks seemed to provide a reasonable amount of energy but frequent rests were necessary. I'd lost considerable weight and had twice sewn tucks in the waistband of my trousers. The trousers were a real nuisance when they sagged. Yet I was convinced that moving at night was my best option. If our own forces had made any gains, I might encounter Japanese forces at any time.

'As twilight deepened I pushed on, crossed one stream, then another. I was in sparse vegetation when I heard a low-flying twin-engine aircraft approaching. I got my flashlight out and when the aircraft was near flashed in Morse code for the first letter of my name.

'I did this a few times. I was certain I'd seen the navigation lights flash in recognition. It did not circle but disappeared north. It could have been RAF or Japanese; no way of knowing.

'Later that night I was trying to pick up a cart track in quite dense bush when I came upon a clearing. I'd just started to cross the clearing when there was a sudden shrieking and screaming of monkeys in the trees to my left. They came down from the trees and spread around the clearing. They seemed quite large, at least two to three feet [60–90 cm] high and one large one came towards me making growling noises. I found some twigs and pebbles, threw them at him. He became even more agitated, jumping around in a menacing way.

'I was starting to panic when I pulled my flashlight from the top of my kit and shone it at the large animal, now about ten feet [3 m] away. As soon as the light went on there was louder screaming and the entire pack rushed for the trees. I lost no time in going in the opposite direction, jumping a hedge into another clearing and then off into more bush. I don't know if they were monkeys or apes but they seemed larger than the monkeys I'd encountered.

'Then I found the cart track and followed it till daylight.

'I was hiding in bush near an open area on the side of a hill when a DC3 came along the valley flying low. I got my metal mirror out and tried to attract attention by the sun's reflection. No response and the DC3 did not return. It was an exciting development. It had a side door open and at such a low altitude that probably meant it was looking for a drop zone.

'It could be that our forces which had been pushing south had made a really great advance and were now south of the Gangaw Valley. I could only speculate.

'After dark I went back to the cart track heading north, more cautious than ever. At about midnight I felt I should be getting close to a village so moved only about a hundred yards [91 m] or so at a time.

'Then I heard voices in the bush. I crept closer, the language was unknown. I crept along the track and saw the glow of fires. Shortly I came to a stream. I was looking for a shallow place to cross when I heard a rattle of stones on the other side of the stream. I ran behind a clump of bushes and crouched on one knee, knife in hand. I remained motionless for quite a time when suddenly there was a splash and clatter of stones.

'A figure with rifle and bayonet extended round the bush. I dived at him and we sprawled on the ground. I lunged with the knife, hitting him on the back but no penetration. He started to roll over. My right hand, my support as I lunged, was on a fair-sized rock. I swung the rock overhead and hit him in the face as he rolled.

'No sound from him. He did not move. I got up, splashed across the stream and went as fast as I could along the track. The track went across open ground. I was on the upgrade of a slight rise when a Japanese soldier appeared walking towards me. He was very close and I felt that to run would be fatal. I slouched by him and as soon as I reached some bush, took cover.

'Almost immediately about twenty or more Japanese came along carrying packs and rifles. Also a couple of bullock carts. I remained in the bush at the side of the track and shortly a large number of Japanese passed by, perhaps a hundred. I moved away from the track into the hills. At daylight I crept back down the track and saw another small group of Japanese pass by. I went back into the hills and found cover for the day.

'The Japanese might be retreating, so friendly forces should be somewhere in the area. I thought as to how I might make safe contact. In dense country, [my] view was very limited so it was impossible to observe troop movements from a distance.

'I thought to avoid the cart track and head across country to the north towards the village of Lessaw. At dusk I started to move. I saw camp fires ahead and decided not to risk trying to pass them. On returning to the track I heard voices, so retreated back to the hills.

'In the next few hours I heard sounds of fighting in the

distance to the north. There was the sound of what might be mortars and also the rattle of automatic weapons. It might be 3 to 4 miles [5–6.5 km] away. I remained in my safe place and during the day all was quiet. I thought to get the last tin of Horlicks opened but it was not in the kit. At any rate there were only six Horlicks left. At about 6 p.m. I ate two Horlicks and a Benzedrine.

'When it was dark I went back to the track. I headed north. I came to a small village and took off boots and socks to make less noise. I walked through. I didn't stop to rest that night and just before daybreak I moved off the track and found cover on the side of a hill. Almost immediately I heard the plodding of animal hoofs, the creak of leather and jingle of chains. I remained hiding.

'During the day I saw DC3s dropping supplies at the east end of the long valley. After dark I finished the Horlicks and took a couple of Benzedrine tablets before I started to move. I did not walk on the track but in the bush in an easterly direction. I did not want to be caught in the open by surprise. The Benzedrine did its work and by daylight I was at the east end of the valley. There had been some gunfire during the night but due to dense growth I could not pinpoint it. It was now quite light and from my position on a ridge I could see two knolls so decided to go in that direction.

'I went down the hill, passed some huts and saw two natives. They saw me but I kept on going.

'I hiked across the valley to the closest knoll and climbed to its top, a good vantage point from which to spot the drop zone if the DC3s came back. Then I heard movement and saw three Indian soldiers coming over the crest of the hill. I started to raise my hands. The soldier nearest me had an automatic weapon at hip level and as I raised my hands he pulled the trigger.

'A swish of bullets around me before I dived behind a tree. I yelled in English, "Do not fire, I'm a British officer."

'Then there was another couple of bursts thudding into the tree and throwing up dirt from the ground. I yelled again, this time in Urdu. No answer. I pulled out my handkerchief, waved it around the tree and shouted again. Still no sound. I jumped up, scrambled down the hill and across the valley to the closest hill and bush. I ran along a ridge for a short distance, then hid under some dead fallen trees. All was quiet the remainder of the day.

'I was in a now-or-never situation. With no Horlicks tablets and feeling let down from the Benzedrine, my energy bursts were getting shorter, I was having to rest more frequently. I didn't think I could make it through the hills to Gangaw.

'In the late afternoon I made a decision. I stripped off to the waist, exposing my white skin, carried my battle-dress top and kit by hand, and started back along the ridge.

'If I encountered Japs I'd have to run or hide but if I came upon our own forces perhaps they'd see a white skin and hold their fire. I walked down into the valley and after a mile [1.5 km] or so heard voices through the bush ahead. I crawled forward and saw a group of natives in a dried-up gully, a dozen men and also women and children. There were cooking pots over fires. I decided to risk making contact. As I scrambled down the gully the women and children ran off, the men remained.

'By sign language I indicated food. Their expressions showed they were apprehensive. I sat down with legs crossed and the men crouched in a semi-circle in front of me. I got out my last small piece of chewing gum, broke it in two, handed a piece to a man who seemed to be in authority. I chewed my piece and he did likewise. He broke into a grin.

'Suddenly they were all smiles and after signs and gestures I was given a bowl of rice. I ate more than I should have. I had a card in my kit with several native dialects in phonetic phrases and tried to converse.

'The only words to trigger a response were UNGLI [Hindi Urdu word meaning finger] and JAPONI. When I repeated Ungli over and over the man pointed to the south-west. By sign language I indicated I wanted him to take me to the Ungli.

'He nodded but indicated that first we should sleep and when the sun came up we would go. I felt uneasy. I got slowly to my feet, indicated we should go now. He nodded. I indicated he should walk ahead of me and took a boy of slight stature with me. A couple of other men trailed behind. I made sure the man saw my hand on my knife.

'We walked down the valley through sparse bush for several miles and came to a stream. About 100 feet [30 m] ahead of me a group of Indian soldiers were washing themselves in a stream: a soldier with a rifle was standing guard on the bank.

'We walked up to him. I said, "Commanding Officer, kidhur hai" [Hindi for hello kid]. He looked at me and nodded to his left. Off we went, natives included. Within half a minute we walked to a shallow ravine where the officers of the 4th/14th Punjabi Regiment were having their evening meal. After explanations and introductions I gave the natives metal rupees from my money belt before they left. I ate more food and was sorry for having done so.

'I cannot remember the Colonel's name but he was most understanding and solicitous as to my wellbeing. He was interested in knowing where I had encountered the Japanese. He said they would break camp at daylight and that I would go by jeep with him to where DC3s were landing with supplies and the main force was located.

'He summoned the three soldiers who had shot at me and they explained they thought I was part of a Jap patrol.

'I bedded down in a shallow slit trench but didn't sleep too well because of fierce stomach cramps At dawn the Colonel gave me a rifle with part of the stock missing, a bandolier of ammunition and suggested we should keep a sharp lookout as Jap stragglers may have been missed.

'We set off in a jeep with an Indian driver, an Indian medical officer and a wounded Chin hillman who had been with the regiment. The Chin was strapped to an overhead stretcher but we soon discarded the stretcher and tied him to the front seat. [The Chin was a Chindit, from a special operations unit organized by the British and Indian armies.]

'The track was extremely rough, we had about 20 miles [32 km] to cover. After a few miles I saw a lot of brown men on the track ahead and they quickly disappeared into the bush. We'd encountered a Chin patrol, part of the V force operating alone in the mountains for more than a year. [The V force was a reconnaissance, intelligence gathering and guerrilla organization organized by British intelligence against Japanese forces.]

'We pressed on and arrived at Tilin where the medical officer dropped me off at a landing strip.

'I approached the pilot of the first DC3 to come in and explained my position. He was very sorry but he had strict orders not to take any passengers. I was astounded. But I was a sad-looking sight with scruffy beard, thin as a bean pole, tattered battle dress but still with wings and rank stripes on my tunic. I ran to a latrine and practically exploded, the first bowel movement I'd had since the third day after I'd bailed out.

'I went back to the strip to try the next aircraft. This time the pilot, an Australian, was very sympathetic and agreed to take me to his destination at Imphal. He told me 28 Squadron was no longer at Kalemyo but 221 Group HQ was nearby.

'On landing I went up to the tower and called Group HQ by landline. Air Commodore Vincent knew every pilot in his group. His aide-de-camp answered the phone and I heard him say, "He says he is Flight Lieutenant Johnson of 28 Squadron". I could hear a voice saying, "Johnson, where the hell is he?" His staff car would be there in a few minutes to pick me up.'

## AFTERWARDS ...

Squadron Leader Bob Johnson's extraordinary three-week ordeal ended that day, 6 February 1943. He remained at HQ until an intelligence officer arrived from Calcutta to debrief him and he returned to 28 Squadron in central Burma after a few days. Several months later he learned he had been awarded a Military Cross. In April, he was sent to visit all forward area squadrons – to lecture on escape and evasion.

After the war he met his wife to be, Shirley Laver, at a Canadian army base. They married and had four sons and one daughter. He worked for many years as an insurance salesman and loss adjuster until retiring in 1977 at Charlottetown, Prince Edward Island, on Canada's eastern shore.

His story is one of many others from the Burma Star Memorial Fund, a charity dedicated to remembering 'The Forgotten Army', the legacy of those who served in the Allied forces through the Burma Campaign of the Second World War.

CHAPTER 7

# THE LAST OF
# THE MANY

B Y THE SUMMER OF 1944, THE war in Europe was reaching
its final stage with the Allied advance through Normandy.
And at this point, the last-ever Hurricane built by Hawker
Aircraft came off the production line.

On 12 August 1944, Hurricane IIC PZ865 left the big Langley
factory in Berkshire. Displayed prominently on its fuselage
were the words: 'The Last of the Many'. The date marked a
formal ceremony and flypast at Langley to mark the end of this
remarkable era – ten years since Sir Sydney Camm had come
up with his proposed Hawker monoplane.

Camm's had been a truly global concept. The Hurricane,
major campaigns aside, flew against the Italians in Abyssinia,
in East Africa, in Iraq (to help suppress pro-Axis unrest) and
in Syria.

Even at the time the last Hurri was being celebrated at Langley
it was still continuing to fly in various roles. It remained in
RAF service in Britain until the end of the Second World War,
testing equipment and weapons, training pilots and producing
weather reports.

The Hurricane's final years witnessed the last events of the war. In June 1944, Hurricane IICs and IVs with 63 Squadron performed reconnaissance around Dieppe in the weeks up to the D-Day landings of 6 June. And, of course, as already noted, Hurricanes still flew, often with outstanding tenacity from the airmen, on the other side of the world in the midst of the Pacific war.

When the Japanese finally accepted the Allies' demand for unconditional surrender on 14 August 1945, following the dropping of the atomic bombs on Hiroshima and Nagasaki, it definitively marked the end of the Second World War.

That August day at Langley was a great event, with a large crowd of Hawker employees, their families and guests – and Sir Sydney Camm seated on a dais in place of honour. The man in the cockpit for the flypast was, of course, George Bulman, the test pilot who had taken the prototype to the air for the first time at Brooklands in November 1935. Widely acknowledged for his work with Hawker, Bulman would soon retire in 1945.

That August day belonged to the Hurricane and its adoring public, the big moment being celebrated widely in print.

'One of the most famous and versatile fighter aircraft in the world, the Hawker Hurricane is nearing the end of its fighting career', trumpeted *The Times* on 14 August 1944.

Describing Bulman's final flypast at Langley, it was equally enthusiastic.

'He zoomed upward in climbing rolls, looping, stalling, flick rolling, coming out of an outside loop to dive and flip within a few feet of the ground, then roaring again almost vertically into the sky.'

Yet this was not quite the end of the Hurricane story. The 'old warrior' PZ865 did not go into RAF service. It was purchased from the then Air Ministry by Hawker Aircraft.

To this day it still takes to the skies each year during the Battle of Britain memorial flight.

## AFTER THE SECOND WORLD WAR

After the war, the demand for reconditioned Hurricanes came from countries like Portugal and Iran (then known as Persia).

Hawker records show that in May and July 1946, seventy Mark IIC machines were on order. In 1947, a dual trainer version of the Hurricane IIC to operate in tropical conditions was produced for the Persian Air Force.

In the decade after the Second World War, several movies portraying the Battle of Britain were produced, mostly to recreate some of the powerful episodes at the beginning of the Second World War. One 1950s film was called *Angels One Five*, directed by George More O'Ferrall, a former Army Liaison Officer during the Battle of Britain. Released in the UK in 1952, it showed the operational life of a typical Hawker Hurricane squadron at an RAF base during the battle. But when setting up to film *Angels One Five* the production company faced a dilemma: they needed airworthy Hurricanes to be used for filming. Where were they?

The last front-line RAF Hurricanes had already been retired from operational service. At the time there were just two flying examples left in Britain: Hurricane IIC PZ865, 'The Last of the Many', which Group Captain Peter Townsend had flown in the King's Cup Air Race in the early 1950s, and IIC LF363, which remained with the RAF – continuously flown in Battle of Britain memorial flights.

In Portugal, however, reconditioned Hurricanes purchased from Hawker remained in operational service. As a result, the producers were able to recruit five Portuguese examples of airworthy Hurricanes for use in the movie.

Portugal had remained neutral during the Second World War. Yet in six months during 1943 and 1944, ninety-seven Hurricanes had been ordered by the Portuguese, all delivered in separate batches, either Mark IIBs or IICs. Regular training sorties, based on techniques developed by the RAF, were often undertaken.

In 1947, Portugal acquired more Hurricanes. Orders were placed with Hawker to supply forty-four Hurricane IICs and a single IIB reconditioned from a batch of fifty at Langley. The first nine arrived in Portugal in April 1947, thirty-six more followed over the next eight months, distributed to the existing Portuguese squadrons.

By the early 1950s, many of the Portuguese Hurricanes had been damaged beyond repair, lost in accidents or withdrawn from service. In 1951, however, there were still fifteen operational Hurricanes and pilots available.

The official invitation from the British Air Ministry to participate in a forthcoming film about the Hurricane's finest hour resulted in five Hurricanes and five Portuguese pilots being selected for flight from Portugal to the UK, where filming was scheduled to take place. The group left Portugal on 12 July 1951, arriving at RAF Tangmere on 16 July.

During the first five days in England, the Portuguese pilots visited RAF Odiham and Fighter Command HQ in London after they had flown their Hurricanes to Hawker's Langley factory for RAF markings created especially for the film.

The first day of filming took place at RAF Kenley on 20 July 1951. The Portuguese pilots were filmed making several flights from Kenley in four aircraft flying over the local area and the Channel. When filming ended, the Portuguese

Hurricanes returned home on 17 August. The film was released in 1952. *Angels One Five* became a British post-war classic.

The Portuguese Hurricanes continued to fly for a short time. Portugal became the last nation to use them operationally. The Hurricane's last flight took place at Sintra in June 1954.

## WHERE ARE THEY NOW?

There are currently an estimated sixteen airworthy Hurris and a number located in museums worldwide.

There is a very good reason for this relatively low figure: as rugged and survivable as the Hurricane was in the days of its early combat, it could not survive as well as the Spitfire, for instance, after the war years.

As a 'gate guardian', at the entrance to RAF stations, for example, an all-metal Spitfire survived well in British weathers. This did not apply to the Hurricane, simply because of its structure. The rear fuselage, fabric covered, and the structure around the canopy, made of wood, when left outside in the British climate, starts to fall apart. As a consequence, for many years the Hurricane never reached any 'restoration to flying' schedule. This problem in preserving and restoring the plane to flying conditions continued for many years. It was not resolved until the 1990s.

The Hurri tail plane, requiring sheets of a very special steel to bend the steel round – a process of rolling to make the tail plane spar – made it difficult to restore, i.e. to source any set of rollers to do this. The cost of making new rollers was prohibitive. So the rusty tail plane spars had a profoundly negative effect on the progress of any restoration efforts.

But in later years the issue gradually started to resolve with improved technology.

Hawker Restoration, the world's leading restorers of the Hurricane, have restored nine Hurricanes (including a recent two-seater plane) and are in the early stages of bringing the total to ten.

Restoring a 1940s Hurri is, of course, a labour of love, dedication, a great deal of time and huge sums of money.

Yet such is the legacy of the remarkable fighter – the plane that so nearly didn't get into the air without the talent and foresight of the men who created her – that its history, as told on these pages, will most likely continue to evolve.

Perhaps its epitaph should echo the words of the ancient Romans: 'Fortune and love favour the brave.' In so many ways, surely those words underline the story of the Hurricane, the plane that won the war?

# ACKNOWLEDGEMENTS

A VERY BIG THANK YOU TO aviation historian Mark Hillier, whose valuable input and enthusiasm are always appreciated. David Coxon at Tangmere Military & Aviation Museum and David Hassard at Kingston Aviation Archive were also extremely helpful for their fascinating insights into the history of the Hurricane.

Sincere thanks too to the publishing team at Michael O'Mara Books, especially Louise Dixon, Senior Editorial Director and Gabriella Nemeth, Senior Editor. Their consistent diligence and support made a huge difference. My gratitude also goes to Mick Oakey at the Aviation Historian, research guru Ray Rose, Abigail Clark and James Brown at Hurricane Heritage, photographer Harvey Mills, Anne Tucker, Anne Holmes, Martin Bisiker at Legasee, author Elinor Florence, Emma Cann of the Burma Star Memorial Fund, Annie O'Brian, RAF Association, Kris Hendrix, RAF Museum, RAF Northolt Polish Museum, Jill Harrison, MOD and the teams at Imperial War Museums, National Archives, Kew as well as everyone at Jubilee Library, Hove Library and the ever helpful Inge and Paul Sweetman, Isobel and Suzanne at City Books, Hove.

# PICTURE CREDITS

Page 8: © IWM / CH 1413 (top); Photo by S. A. Devon / Imperial War Museums via Getty Images (bottom)

Page 9: GBM Historical Images / Shutterstock (both)

Page 10: © IWM / CM 4957 (top); © IWM / TR 866 (centre); Photo by P. H. F. Tovey / Imperial War Museums via Getty Images (bottom)

Page 11: © IWM / CNA 3035 (top); © IWM / CH 1570 (bottom)

Page 12: © IWM / ME(RAF) 1260 (top); Bettmann / Getty Images (bottom)

Page 13: De Luan / Alamy (top); © IWM / Documents.11775 (centre & bottom)

Page 14: © IWM / MH 13763 (top left); © IWM / CH 1539 (top right); © IWM HU 128279 (centre); Photography by Harvey Mills (bottom)

Page 15: Photographs by Abigail Clark and James Brown, Hurricane Heritage

Page 16: Darren Harbar Photography, www.darrenharbar.co.uk

# FURTHER READING

Bishop, Patrick, *Fighter Boys*, HarperCollins, 2020

Coxon, David and Byron, Reginald, *Tangmere: An Authorised History*, Grub Street Publishing, 2014

McKinstry, Leo, *Hurricane: Victor of the Battle of Britain*, John Murray, 2010

Overy, Richard, *The Battle of Britain: Myth and Reality*, 2010

Richey, Paul, *Fighter Pilot*, The History Press, 2016

Stewart, Adrian, *Hurricane*, Canelo, 2021

The story of Bill Millington and that of other Australian Battle of Britain heroes in this book are abridged accounts from *Australia's Few and the Battle of Britain* by Kristen Alexander.

# INDEX